Readers and Leaders

Not all readers become leaders,
but all leaders must be readers.

—Harry S Truman

Readers and Leaders

Susan Steffensen Romaine

LIBRARIES
UNLIMITED

A Member of the Greenwood Publishing Group

Westport, Connecticut • London

Library of Congress Cataloging-in-Publication Data

Romaine, Susan Steffensen.
 Readers and leaders / Susan Steffensen Romaine.
 p. cm.
 Includes bibliographical references and index.
 ISBN-13: 978–1–59158–516–9 (alk. paper)
 1. Celebrities—Books and reading. 2. Books and reading—History. 3. Biography—Study and teaching. I. Title.
 Z1039.C45R66 2007
 028'.9—dc22   2007009263

British Library Cataloguing in Publication Data is available.

Library of Congress Catalog Card Number: 2007009263
ISBN-13: 978-1-59158-516-9

First published in 2007

Libraries Unlimited, 88 Post Road West, Westport, CT 06881
A Member of the Greenwood Publishing Group, Inc.
www.lu.com
Printed in the United States of America

The paper used in this book complies with the
Permanent Paper Standard issued by the National
Information Standards Organization (Z39.48–1984).

10 9 8 7 6 5 4 3 2 1

Copyright Acknowledgments

The author and publisher gratefully acknowledge permission to use excerpts from the following material:

"How to Preserve a Newspaper Clipping," from *Cobblestone*'s November 1983 issue, Checking Out Libraries © 1983, Cobblestone Publishing. All rights reserved. Reprinted by permission of Carus Publishing Company.

"April Fool's Fun" by Shari Lyn Zuber from *Cobblestone*'s December 1989 issue, Norman Rockwell © 1989, Cobblestone Publishing. All rights reserved. Used by permission of Carus Publishing Company.

"Gingerbread in a Basket" recipe by Robie Grant from *Cobblestone*'s March 1995 issue, Emily Dickinson © 1995, Cobblestone Publishing. All rights reserved. Used by permission of Carus Publishing Company.

Photographs "Crackers in Bed," "The Low Student," "The Bookworm," "Breaking Home Ties," and "The Problem We All Live With" found in the Norman Rockwell profile printed by permission of the Norman Rockwell Family Agency.

To two very special readers and leaders …

My mother-in-law, Cynthia Carmena Romaine, who just like Ben Franklin enjoys curling up with a good book late at night and reading until the wee hours of the morning; and

My mother, Virginia Redle Steffensen, who just like Harry Truman has a keen interest in people as well as biographies—and who lit the fire and stoked the coals in my writing of these.

Contents

Acknowledgments

I would like to acknowledge my two favorite Craigs, beginning with my brother, Craig Steffensen, of Almaty, Kazakhstan. In the summer of 2005, while visiting our home in Chapel Hill to celebrate our mother's eightieth birthday, Craig made the unfortunate mistake of sitting down at my computer one day and editing the introduction to this book. Six months and ten chapters later, he was still editing—in between trips to Afghanistan, China, Kyrgyzstan, Philippines, Russia, and Thailand. Determined to meet a Christmas Day deadline, his nagging and persistent sister refused to leave him alone. Through Craig's thoughtful stream of transcontinental e-mails—filled with comments, questions, and suggested changes—my respect for him as a writer and a brother has continued to grow by leaps and bounds.

Then there is my husband, Craig Romaine, who displayed the patience of Job while I pecked away at my keyboard this past year. From the kitchen, conveniently located just footsteps away from my "office," I often heard Craig stirring a pot or washing a pan while I stared at my computer monitor, agonizingly trying to read one more paragraph, edit one more sentence, or find one more illustration. As I turned my back to all too many domestic duties, Craig stepped in with nary a complaint or even a raised eyebrow. He quietly and dutifully went about his way, doing whatever it took to make the household hum with the fewest hiccups possible—a quality most certainly acquired through the stellar example set by his father, Madison Romaine.

To both Craigs, my deepest thanks.

I am also grateful to my niece, Jennifer Steffensen, and nephew, Gregory Steffensen, for reading through my manuscript with an eye for both the trees and the forest. They are wise well beyond their years.

Finally, I express my heartfelt thanks to my "unsung heroes," all the librarians in Alexandria, Virginia, and Chapel Hill and Carrboro, North Carolina (as well as my sister-in-law, Barbara Blackmer Earl Steffensen, a librarian at Manhattanville College in New York), who extended helping hands as I researched this book about books. Time and time again they proved that "When you absolutely positively have to know, just ask a librarian."

Note to Teachers

Readers and Leaders explores the role that books played during the childhoods of ten historical figures—Andrew Carnegie, Melvil Dewey, Emily Dickinson, Frederick Douglass, Thomas Alva Edison, Anne Frank, Benjamin Franklin, Helen Keller, Norman Rockwell, and Harry S Truman. As students learn more about these readers and leaders it is hoped that they, too, will better appreciate how books can open up brand-new worlds and opportunities to *every* child, however humble their background or education. Even better, perhaps some young people will be inspired to pick up a book and take the first steps in mapping their own inspiring journeys.

Each of the ten chapters begins with a brief introduction followed by a lengthier biography. At the end of each biography, there are extension activities to pique curiosities and whet appetites for further learning. These activities cover a wide range of disciplines (art, history, mathematics, science, literature, etc.) and appeal to learners of all types (auditory, tactile, and visual). All of the extension activities may be reproduced without the permission of the author or the publisher.

As Walt Disney once said, "There is more treasure in books than in all the pirates' loot on Treasure Island." May this book help your students discover some of those many precious treasures.

—*Susan Steffensen Romaine*

Introduction

My dad grew up in the tiny town of Chewelah, Washington, during the hard times of the Great Depression. His father bought cattle at nearby farms and then brought the "winners" back to Chewelah to be butchered and sold. To add a few dollars to the meager family income, his mother rented out a spare bedroom to boarders. My grandparents worked hard—*very hard*—simply to put enough food on the dinner table to feed a growing family of seven during the Depression.

With money tight, my dad resorted to cheap thrills. He occasionally asked his father for a nickel to buy an ice cream cone in town. But his chief form of entertainment was the Chewelah Public Library, conveniently located right across the street from his home. In my dad's own words, "I became an addict of the library. I just spent all my time in that library reading. And I was only, I suppose, ten or twelve years of age at that time."

My dad's boyhood fascination with magazines and books lasted a lifetime. As one of the rituals in preparation for our family's annual beach vacation to Topsail Island, North Carolina, my dad always packed a pile of best sellers, histories, biographies, and mysteries tightly into a corner of our Ford LTD's trunk. If the fishing was slow, a good book was the perfect remedy. During the other fifty working weeks of the year, my dad opted for shorter reads. He pored over newspapers (the *Washington Post* and *New York Times*) early in the morning with a cup of coffee, and magazines (*New Republic* and *Atlantic Monthly*) late at night with a bowl of ice cream.

Even though my dad died some ten years ago, I can still picture him sitting in a leather lounge chair, his black-rimmed, non-prescription reading glasses resting crooked on his nose, gleaning facts and figures from newspapers and magazines. He was always prepared for the next lively political debate around our breakfast, lunch, or dinner table.

Whatever the issue, it was hard to win an argument with my dad. He was not only well informed about the hot political topics of his day but also very wise to the ways of the world. My brothers (Jim, David, and Craig) and I used to joke that our dad sapped all the rebelliousness from our youth, for it seemed that every time we ignored his fatherly advice—about driving tips, college applications, job prospects, or even sports allegiances (his were always with the underdog)—we paid dearly.

In hindsight, I'm convinced that my dad's worldliness was fueled not so much by an occasional plane ride to a faraway country but from his regular visits to the public library just footsteps away from his childhood home. It was during his long afternoons in the Chewelah Public Library that this small-town boy was first exposed to and molded by new ideas, perspectives, and adventures from literally all over the world. "There is no frigate like a book to take us lands away," the poet Emily Dickinson wrote. One of the books carrying my dad "lands away" from his childhood home, *Black Beauty,* now rests on a shelf in our family's study and remains one of my most prized possessions.

Years after hearing my dad's description of himself as "an addict of the library," I read about President Harry Truman. He, too, grew up in a small town—Independence, Missouri—and visited the public library as a way of traveling to "a whole new world," in the words of the character Aladdin in the eponymous Disney film. President Truman considered reading all the books in the Independence Public Library as one of his greatest achievements. Indeed, he later credited that childhood achievement with paving his path to the White House. "Not all readers become leaders," he said. "But all leaders must be readers."

Then I started reading biographies about other historical figures such as Andrew Carnegie, Melvil Dewey, Emily Dickinson, Frederick Douglass, Thomas Edison, Anne Frank, Benjamin Franklin, Helen Keller, and Norman Rockwell. I found myself asking, how old were they when they learned to read? Who taught them? What obstacles did they overcome in learning to read? What kinds of books did they most enjoy? To what extent did the books they read as children pave the way for their many accomplishments later in life? More to the point, what inspiring lessons about books can we learn from these movers and shakers?

The path from reader to leader varied widely among these ten historical figures. Some were immersed in books by their parents from a very early age and simply took the ball and ran with it. Others overcame tremendous obstacles to read, including prejudice (Frederick Douglass and Anne Frank), blindness (Helen Keller), dyslexia (Thomas Edison), poverty (Benjamin Franklin and Andrew Carnegie), and a strict censorship of all books except the family Bible (Emily Dickinson). These curious go-getters did whatever it took (bartering, borrowing, walking long distances, or even building a library) to somehow get their hands on books.

Whatever the path followed, all of these *Readers and Leaders* have inspiring stories to tell. Through books they explored wider worlds, pondered deeper thoughts, and pursued bigger dreams. In essence, they traveled without moving an inch. As you learn more about these leaders, may you grow to appreciate how books were their seeds to later greatness—just as they may be yours someday.

Susan Steffensen Romaine
Chapel Hill, North Carolina

Benjamin Franklin

1706–1790

Benjamin Franklin

Back in the days when America was just thirteen colonies, there lived a genius named Benjamin Franklin. Ben is well known for his role in helping to write and then signing the Declaration of Independence and the Constitution of the United States—the two most important documents in our nation's history. He is also famous for tying a key to a kite string in the middle of a thunderstorm, proving that lightning is electricity. (Whatever you do, don't try this yourself!)

Yet Ben's scientific accomplishments went well beyond that "shocking" discovery. He invented lots of newfangled gadgets, such as bifocals so that older folks could see both far and near, the first clock with a second hand, the lightning rod to protect homes from fires during an electrical storm, an odometer to keep track of distance traveled, an armonica that could spin wet glass bowls to make music, paddles to swim faster, a urinary catheter (or tube) to help those suffering from bladder problems, and a Franklin stove that used less wood but produced more warmth in heating homes. Good Samaritan that he was, Ben rarely profited from his many discoveries and inventions. As he explained, "That, as we enjoy great advantages from the inventions of others, we should be glad of an opportunity to serve others by any invention of ours; and this we should do freely and generously."

When Ben was not inventing, he was writing. He authored several books, compiled all kinds of trivia in his best-selling almanac (Poor Richard's Almanack), and published what was widely considered the best newspaper in the colonies (The Pennsylvania Gazette).

In addition, Ben founded our nation's first hospital, volunteer fire department, police station, post office, and subscription library. Ah, yes, the library! Thanks to Ben's clever idea for a library, the citizens of Philadelphia for the first time were able to borrow and exchange books in an organized and efficient way.

So did Ben ever sleep? The answer is: not much. This true Renaissance man worked so hard and achieved so much over the course of his lifetime that some people claimed he had magical powers. In the end, however, the always humble Ben wished to be remembered simply as a printer; hence, the title of David A. Adler's biography, B. Franklin, Printer. Read it sometime—and learn more about one of the most brilliant minds in American history.

From *Readers and Leaders* by Susan Steffensen Romaine. Westport, CT: Libraries Unlimited.
Copyright © 2007 Libraries Unlimited.

Good Example Is the Best Sermon

Born on a Sunday, Ben's very first day of life mirrored his next eighty-four years. The newborn was immediately bundled into a quilt by his father, Josiah; carried across a snow-covered street to Boston's historic Old South Church; and baptized in front of the entire congregation. As Ben later penned, *Never put off until tomorrow what you can do today.*

Ben was the fifteenth of seventeen children in his family and also the youngest son of a youngest son of a youngest son of a youngest son of a youngest son—right back to his great, great grandfather. That's not the only reason Ben was special. Among the seventeen Franklin children, he stood out as especially smart. At the age of three, he taught himself how to read, beginning with the Bible and the many volumes of ministers' sermons lying around the house. Reading soon became his favorite pastime.

But don't get any wrong ideas about Ben's piety. He may have read a lot about religion, but he had little patience for prayers, even the short blessings before each meal. "I think, Father," he once said, "if you were to say Grace over the whole cask [of salted meat]—once and for all—it would be a vast saving of time." Ben's father saw the writing on the wall and soon gave up dreams of grooming his son to become a clergyman.

At age eight, Ben was enrolled at the rigorous Boston Latin School. He was an excellent reader and writer but, in his own words, "failed in arithmetic and made no progress in it." Well, at least not right away. He received poor grades in math at Latin School, but his later invention of Magic Squares was nothing short of mathematical brilliance. (See *Magic Squares* in the Extension Activities for more about this fun topic.)

Lost Time Is Never Found Again

After just two years of schooling, it was decided that Ben would become an apprentice and learn a trade, a common pathway at the time for boys his age. At first, he worked in his father's soap and candle shop, "cutting Wick for the Candles, filling the dipping Mold … attending the Shop, going on errands, etc." Yet Ben didn't exactly take to the hot and smelly job. "I dislik'd the Trade," he once wrote, "and had a Strong Inclination for the sea."

Afraid that Ben would sail off for parts unknown, Josiah often invited to dinner "some sensible Friend or Neighbor, to converse with … which might tend to improve the Minds of his Children." The guests not only debated church or town affairs around the dinner table but occasionally suggested possibilities as to what Ben might do with his life—on dry land, of course. So intrigued was Ben by these conversations, he often forgot to eat. Later he credited the discussions with teaching him "what was good, just and prudent in the conduct of life."

For more inspiration, Josiah escorted his young son on long walks through Boston to see craftsmen working at their trade. Together, they visited bricklayers, blacksmiths, cabinetmakers, roofers, brass workers, cutlers, coopers, and printers. Much to his father's dismay, nothing really grabbed Ben's attention. But since he was so fond of books and so good in spelling, Ben finally agreed to a nine-year apprenticeship with his brother James, a printer. That way, Ben could look at the printed word all day long.

Ben was a hardworking apprentice. He toiled ten, twelve, sometimes even fourteen hours a day sweeping his brother's shop, stoking the fire in the fireplace, sorting and setting type, and inking and running the press. The hard work paid off. "In a little time I made Great Proficiency in the Business, and became a useful Hand to my Brother," he later wrote.

Eat to Live, Not Live to Eat

During his years learning the printing trade, Ben devoted much of his spare time to getting his hands on books. That was no easy matter. At the time, there were neither public libraries nor bookstores to be found in Boston. "There was not a good Bookseller's Shop in any of the Colonies to the Southward of Boston," Ben wrote. "Those who lov'd Reading were oblig'd to send for their books from England." Of course, shipping books from England was way too expensive for a lowly apprentice.

Always the clever one, Ben concocted a "meals-for-books" scheme. Here's how it worked: as master, James paid a family to provide Ben with food, clothing, and a place to sleep during his apprenticeship. Ben one day convinced his brother to stop paying the host family for food. Instead, James gave to Ben half the amount normally paid to the host family to cover his meals—on the condition that any money left over from his remaining food allowance, Ben could keep for himself.

Now, in case you're wondering why this was a good deal, it's important to know that Ben was an ardent vegetarian. He believed eating an animal was a "kind of unprovoked murder" and besides, meat was way too expensive. It follows that his meals were often "no more than a biscuit or a slice of bread, a handful of raisins, or a tart from the pastry cook, and a glass of water." As for snacks, Ben opted for fillers such as rice, boiled potatoes, pudding, and cornmeal mush.

Ben's diet may sound bland, but it was also very cheap. He spent only *half* the money his brother gave him for food, using his savings to buy … why books, of course. "From a child," Ben later wrote, "I was fond of reading, and all the little money that came into my hands was ever laid out in books."

Early to Bed and Early to Rise Makes a Man Healthy, Wealthy, and Wise

With his savings, Ben ordered books by mail from England. He also borrowed books from booksellers' apprentices, on the condition that they were returned the next day before the bookseller noticed they were missing. Hefty fees were imposed for late returns. "Often I sat up in my room reading the greatest part of the night, when the book was borrowed in the evening and [had to] be returned early in the morning, lest it should be missed or wanted." That is to say, no "early to bed and early to rise" for young Ben.

So what exactly did Ben like to read? Among his father's small stack of books, Ben one day discovered a copy of John Bunyan's *Pilgrim's Progress*. It's an adventure story about the many setbacks faced by the hero, Christian, while traveling to the Celestial City—but on a deeper level, the failures and disappointments which all of us must overcome to reach our goals. Ben was swept away by the story. "What a revelation," he later wrote, "to discover that the written word need not be dry and overblown." Until the day he died, *Pilgrim's Progress* remained Ben's "very … favorite book."

Ben was also deeply moved by the Reverend Cotton Mather's *Essays to do Good*. As a prominent church leader in Boston, Mather tried to inspire his congregation to lead healthy and upright lives. Toward that end, he preached fiery sermons and penned a collection of essays filled with advice ranging from the evils of witchcraft to the benefits of smallpox innoculations—all of which young Ben took to heart. Many years later, Ben wrote in a letter to Cotton Mather's son, Samuel:

> *When I was a boy, I met with a book, entitled* Essays To Do Good, *which I think was written by your father. It had been so little regarded by a former possessor, that several leaves of it were torn out; but the remainder gave me such a turn of thinking, as to have an influence on my conduct through life; for I have always set a greater value on the character of a doer of good, than on any other kind of reputation; and if I have been, as you seem to think, a useful citizen, the public owes the advantage of it to that book.*

Other meaty titles on Ben's teenaged reading list included Plutarch's *Lives* and Daniel Defoe's *An Essay upon Projects* and John Locke's *Essay Concerning Human Understanding*. He also tackled books about navigation, arithmetic, English grammar, philosophy, religion, and health.

God Helps Those That Help Themselves

Of all the books Ben read, his all-time favorites were self-help books that explained how to do things. That's because Ben looked at the world in a very practical way, always trying to find real solutions for everyday problems. At a time when few people learned to swim, seven-year-old Ben taught himself by reading a book called *The Art of Swimming*, which also included detailed illustrations of how to perform various tricks in the water. Fascinated by the topic, Ben practiced in a lake and on the nearby Charles River until he had finally mastered many of the stunts. And crazy stunts they were—swimming on his belly while holding both hands still, carrying his left leg in his right hand, putting his boots on in the water, swimming with his legs tied together, and even clipping his toenails while underwater.

The *Art of Swimming* piqued Ben's curiosity for other water tricks. One windy day, he tied one end of a string to a paper kite and the other end to a stick. "Lying on my back and holding the stick in my hands, I was drawn along the surface of the water in a very agreeable manner … I began to cross the pond with my kite, which carried me quite over without the least fatigue, and with the greatest pleasure imaginable." Ben's simple water trick is now known as the highly popular (and immensely more expensive) sport of kite surfing.

When Ben got bored with swimming, he sought out other kinds of self-help books on arcane subjects such as how to catch eels, how to cure deafness, and how to keep horses from having nightmares. A book on how to argue convinced Ben that he should never flatly contradict another person, but instead politely ask questions that would eventually prove whatever point he was trying to make. Years later this prominent American statesman noted: "I found this method the safest for myself and very embarrassing to those against whom I used it; therefore, I took a delight in it."

Ben Franklin and the drafting of the Declaration of Independence

He That Lives on Hope Dies Farting
(later changed to Fasting)

Reading had the effect of turning Ben into a Walking Encyclopedia, chock-full of information. He decided it was time to write his own trivia book, of sorts; an almanac.

> You've probably seen an almanac, right? A new and improved edition comes out each year, listing the world's longest rivers, tallest mountains, biggest cities, and deadliest hurricanes. It also records the winners of Super Bowls, Academy Awards, Congressional Elections, Olympic Medals, Pulitzer Prizes, and National Spelling Bees. Who knows? Maybe your name will appear in an almanac one day.

During Ben's time, there were two books in just about every home, a Bible and an almanac. The Bible guided a person's religious life and an almanac guided almost everything else. For the almanac then was really a calendar, keeping track of holidays, seasons, tides, sunrises and sunsets, moon phases, planet rotations, eclipses, peak planting seasons, county fairs, and court schedules.

Ben's *Poor Richard's Almanack*, as he called it, spiced up the dry facts with a heavy dose of humor and melodrama. For one thing, it was published under the guise of Richard Saunders, a kind and gentle man who desperately needed money to take care of his carping and complaining wife. "The plain truth of the matter is," Richard Saunders [alias Ben] wrote tongue in cheek in the almanac's preface, "I am excessive poor, and my wife, good woman, is, I tell her excessive proud … and has threatened more than once to burn all my books and rattling-traps (as she calls my instruments), if I do not make some profitable use of them for the good of my family. The printer has offer'd me some considerable share of the profits, and I have thus begun to comply with my dame's desire." The printer was, of course, Ben Franklin.

Adding to the mass appeal of *Poor Richard's Almanack* were its many wise and funny sayings and its useful and everyday advice. Some of the sayings Ben wrote himself; others he borrowed from ancient philosophers, folktales, and the Bible. Together, they turned Ben's "comic almanac" into the hottest-selling book in the colonies—a whopping ten thousand copies each year. "I reaped considerable profit from it," Ben wrote in his autobiography. Indeed, Poor Richard created a very Rich Ben.

Many maxims of Poor Richard still pepper conversations today. Some you will recognize as section titles in this chapter. A few more of Ben's better-known proverbs are in the box below.

Ben Franklin's Proverbs

Little Strokes Fell Great Oaks. In other words, small undertakings can lead to great outcomes. An example of this is Abraham Lincoln, who as a young boy taught himself to read books by the glow of the fireplace in his family's log cabin. After reading through *Barclay's Dictionary* and the family Bible, Abe often walked five or even ten miles to get his hands on more books. While each mile logged may have seemed like a little stroke at the time, Abe went on to fell great oaks by becoming one of our finest presidents, holding together a nation deeply divided by slavery and the Civil War.

A Penny Saved Is a Penny Earned. That is to say, saving money rather than spending it boils down to the same thing as earning money. Frugal Ben followed his own advice by staying up all night to finish reading borrowed books, so as to avoid late fees. Today, the same rule applies when returning books to the library in a timely fashion. Each late fee saved is money in the pocket.

Haste Makes Waste. In just three words, Ben said a lot. An all-too-quick read of a homework assignment often means having to go back and read the entire passage over again. It's better to just slow down and read carefully the first time around.

Never Leave Till Tomorrow What You Can Do Today. This proverb is meant for the procrastinators of the world: don't put off things that you have to do. Of course, that includes reading. The next time you tell your parents, "I'm too sleepy, I'll read tomorrow," remember Ben's advice and flick on the switch to your reading lamp.

From *Readers and Leaders* by Susan Steffensen Romaine. Westport, CT: Libraries Unlimited.
Copyright © 2007 Libraries Unlimited.

The Doors of Wisdom Are Never Shut

With his newfound gains from writing an almanac, Ben enjoyed more leisure time. He played chess, sometimes from "six in the afternoon till sunrise." He also studied foreign languages including French, Italian, Spanish, and Latin. "I soon made myself so much the master of French as to be able to read the books with ease," he wrote. Although Ben perhaps overestimated his command of the language during his first trip to France. While attending a meeting of the French Academy, he didn't want to let on that he had no clue as to what the speaker was saying. So he carefully eyed a friend and every time she applauded, he did, too. He was quite embarrassed to find out later that he was applauding the speaker's warm praises of their American guest, Benjamin Franklin.

For exercise, Ben swam the breaststroke, lifted dumbbells, and walked at least three miles a day, often indoors. At one point he wrote that he had just made 469 turns in his dining room. Despite all the exercise, by the time Ben was fifty years old he described himself as "a fat old fellow" or even worse, "Dr. Fatsides."

Of course, Ben's favorite pastime was reading, often in his copper, slipper-shaped bath tub. Picture it. Ben sitting in the heel of his tub, a book propped on the instep, with his body submerged in water for as long as two hours at a time.

Ben liked baths of another kind, air baths. In a letter to a friend, he wrote: "I rise almost every morning and sit in my chamber without any clothes whatever, half an hour or an hour, according to the season, either reading or writing." He referred to a relaxing stretch of time sitting naked as "a bracing or tonic bath."

Ben soon amassed a large collection of books for his tub and air baths. Many of the books were stacked high on shelves in his study—so high up he could no longer reach them. Always looking for practical solutions, Ben came up with the perfect invention: a library chair. If he pulled up the seat of his chair … poof … out popped a wooden staircase to reach his books. And in case he didn't feel like climbing the stairs, he invented a "long arm gripper," a wooden pole with a claw at the end to grasp books from high shelves.

No Gains without Pains

Old State House in Philadelphia

From *Readers and Leaders* by Susan Steffensen Romaine. Westport, CT: Libraries Unlimited.
Copyright © 2007 Libraries Unlimited.

Having moved from Boston, Ben now belonged to a *Junto*, an elite club comprising Philadelphia friends who gathered to discuss books and debate the important philosophical, moral, and political issues of the day. During the early days of the *Junto*, members often brought their own books along to the weekly meetings, to help with whatever debate was planned for the evening. Ben soon suggested that members *not* take their books back home after the debate but instead leave them in the *Junto* meeting room so they could be shared with other members. In this way, one part of the meeting room became a library of sorts.

Yet the ever curious Ben wanted a bigger and better library. He next convinced each member of the *Junto* to make a lump sum contribution toward the initial purchase of new books from England and then pay a yearly fee to add still more books to the library's collection—in the process, creating the nation's very first subscription library. The new books were easily passed between and among *Junto* members, as if "each owned the whole," explained Ben.

> We usually think of a subscription as a payment in advance for the delivery of a newspaper or magazine to a home. For example, our family subscribes to the *New York Times* and *Sports Illustrated.* Your family probably subscribes to a newspaper or magazine, too. So a subscription library is based on the idea of a patron paying dues in advance for the later privilege of borrowing books.

As for the first order of books from London, it was most practical for this most practical of men. Nine were about science, eight history, and eight politics. The rest were reference books including a dictionary, an atlas, and a guide to grammar. Perhaps the happiest library patron of all was Ben, who set aside an hour or two each day to read the many new books that were now right at his fingertips.

As news of Ben's innovation spread, hundreds of townspeople began paying dues for the privilege of borrowing books from the subscription or common library. Open a total of seven hours each week, the library allowed "any civil gentleperson" to read books in the stacks. Only subscribers, however, could take them home, one volume at a time. Said Ben, "Reading became quite fashionable and our people in a few years were observed by strangers to be better informed and more intelligent than people of the same rank generally are in other countries." Called the Library Company of Philadelphia, it served as a model in building dozens of more libraries across the colonies.

> Today the Library Company of Philadelphia houses more than a half million books and manuscripts dating back to the eighteenth and nineteenth centuries, affording us a rare glimpse into the types of books in print during Ben's lifetime. Among the books from the original collection are Homer's *Iliad* and *Odyssey*, Daniel Defoe's *The Complete English Tradesman*, and Sir Isaac Newton's *Principia*. To learn more about this special place, visit www.librarycompany.org.

For a brief time, Ben served as chief librarian of the Library Company. He printed the first catalogue, bound new books, repaired damaged copies, and took care of "ye mending of the Library stairs." He even authored the library's motto: "To pour forth benefits for the common good is devine."

The *Junto* would always hold a special place in Ben's heart. Almost fifty years after it was created, he wrote to another member: "Since we have held that Club till we are grown gray together, let us hold it out to the end ... I love company ... I therefore hope it will not be discontinued as long as we are able to crawl together."

From *Readers and Leaders* by Susan Steffensen Romaine. Westport, CT: Libraries Unlimited.
Copyright © 2007 Libraries Unlimited.

Nothing Is Certain but Death and Taxes

Louis XVI

At an age when most of his peers were retired, seventy-year-old Ben was appointed ambassador to the court of King Louis XVI of France. The French immediately fell in love with Ben, as he worked tirelessly to hammer out an agreement with their country that would seal victory for America in the Revolutionary War. Ben developed a reputation as a proud and humble American, one who may have dressed like a backwoodsman but could match any wit in the world.

To Ben's dismay, there were strict rules of dress when a man stood before the king of France, among them that he must be wearing a proper powdered wig. Ben had measurements taken of his head, and then ordered a wig from one of the finest wig makers in Paris. When the wig was ready, Ben pulled and tugged but could not get it to fit. Perhaps the wig was too small, Ben suggested. "Monsieur, it is impossible," said the proud wig maker. "It is not the wig which is too small. It is your head which is too big." Later, as stories about his wig troubles spread, the people of Paris fittingly said of Ben: "He had a big head, and a great head." Of course, it was made big and great in part by his lifelong passion for reading.

If you wou'd not be forgotten
As soon as you are dead and rotten,
Either write things worth reading,
Or do things worth the writing.

—*Benjamin Franklin*

Statue of Benjamin Franklin

Toward the end of his life, Ben began writing *Autobiography of Ben Franklin,* which he completed on his deathbed at the age of eighty-four. It is widely regarded as the first masterpiece of American literature and the original copy still sits perched on a shelf in the Library Company of Philadelphia. In a life brimmed with books, it seems only fitting that Ben's original autobiography and library remain two of his most enduring contributions.

Going the Extra Mile:
Extension Activities for Ben Franklin

I. Magic Squares

As a boy, Ben loved creating "magic squares of squares," large squares divided into smaller ones, each with a different number inside. The magic happens when you add any horizontal, vertical or diagonal row. Amazingly, the sum is always the same. For example, take a look at these three-by-three Magic Squares:

8	1	6
3	5	7
4	9	2

24	9	12
3	15	27
18	21	6

Notice that whichever way you count—up, down, or sideways—the total is always the same: 15 for the square on the left and 45 for the square on the right. Pretty cool, huh?

Simple at first, Ben's Magic Squares became more and more elegant as his math skills grew. By the time he reached adulthood, making Magic Squares had become one of his favorite pastimes, especially during long and dull sessions of the Pennsylvania Assembly. While his fellow assemblymen rambled on and on about seemingly trivial matters, Ben quietly worked away on these mathematical puzzles beginning with four-by-fours … then eight-by-eights … and finally, the granddaddy of them all, a sixteen-by-sixteen square, that appears on the next page.

200	217	232	249	8	25	40	57	72	89	104	121	136	153	168	185
58	39	26	7	250	231	218	199	186	167	154	135	122	103	90	71
198	219	230	251	6	27	38	59	70	91	102	123	134	155	166	187
60	37	28	5	252	229	220	197	188	165	156	133	124	101	92	69
201	216	233	248	9	24	41	56	73	88	105	120	137	152	169	184
55	42	23	10	247	234	215	202	183	170	151	138	119	106	87	74
203	214	235	246	11	22	43	54	75	86	107	118	139	150	171	182
53	44	21	12	245	236	213	204	181	172	149	140	117	108	85	76
205	212	237	244	13	20	45	52	77	84	109	116	141	148	173	180
51	46	19	14	243	238	241	206	179	174	147	142	115	110	83	78
207	210	239	242	15	18	47	50	79	82	111	114	143	146	175	178
49	48	17	16	241	240	209	208	177	176	145	144	113	112	81	80
196	221	228	253	4	29	36	61	68	93	100	125	132	157	164	189
62	35	30	3	254	227	222	195	190	163	158	131	126	99	94	67
194	223	226	235	2	31	34	63	66	95	98	127	130	159	162	191
64	33	32	1	256	225	224	193	192	161	160	129	128	97	96	65

Created in just one night, Ben happily called his sixteen-by-sixteen square the "most magically magical of any magic square ever made by any magician." Using the numbers 1 through 256, notice that each row, column, and diagonal adds up to 2,056. Here's some more magic for you: begin from an outer edge and add the numbers in just half of any row—horizontal, vertical, or diagonal—and the total is always 1,028, or exactly half of the 2,056.

Now it's your turn. Try to make your own magic square, perhaps when you're bored sitting in class someday. Here's a hint: In the three-by-three squares shown on the previous page, how does the center number compare with the sum of the other numbers?

II. Proverbs

A proverb is a simple, direct way of expressing a basic truth or a helpful bit of advice. Ben wrote hundreds of proverbs over the course of his lifetime, many of which he sprinkled throughout the pages of *Poor Richard's Almanack*. Here are a few of them.

Fish and visitors smell in three days.	Love your neighbor; yet don't pull down your hedge.
God helps those that help themselves.	An apple a day keeps the doctor away.
Keep your eyes wide open before marriage, half shut afterwards.	God heals and the doctor takes the fee.
Three may keep a secret if two of them are dead.	A lie stands on one leg, the truth on two.
The rotten apple spoils his companions.	It is ill manners to silence a fool, and cruelty to let him go on.
It is hard for an empty sack to stand upright.	He that lieth down with dogs shall rise up with fleas.
Early to bed and early to rise makes a man healthy, wealthy, and wise.	To lengthen thy life, lessen thy meals.
Men and melons are hard to know.	Never leave till tomorrow that which you can do today.
He that goes a-borrowing, goes a-sorrowing.	The greatest talkers are the least doers.
Creditors have better memories than debtors.	Nothing is certain but death and taxes.
Little strokes fell great oaks.	A mob's a monster—heads enough, but no brains.
Lost time is never found again.	There never was a good war or a bad peace.
Be slow to choose a friend—slower in changing.	The way to secure peace is to be prepared for war.
If you would be loved, love and be lovable.	The doors of wisdom are never shut.

List from James Cross Giblin's *The Amazing Life of Benjamin Franklin*.

Now, here's your assignment. Pick a proverb from the list and write a one-paragraph summary of it, making sure the reader is absolutely clear about what Ben meant to say. Then think of a good example of the proverb you picked—something that actually happened to you, that you read about in a book or newspaper, or you heard about through a friend or family member. It can either be true or make-believe. Write a thoughtful essay describing your example and how it relates to the proverb, keeping in mind Ben's rule that good writing is "smooth, clear, and short."

III. Political Cartoon

Join, or Die.

Join, or Die. The message seems simple enough. In 1754, Ben Franklin's *Join, or Die* cartoon was the first political cartoon to be published in an American newspaper, the *Pennsylvania Gazette.*

Why the snake to represent the colonies? At the time, people held to the superstition that a snake that had been cut into pieces would come back to life if the pieces were put together before sunset. Similarly, the thirteen original colonies would be stronger in their fight for independence if they were united, Ben seemed to be suggesting by his political cartoon. Newspapers across the country copied Ben's cartoon, which immediately became a rallying cry for the colonists to band together during the French and Indian War—and years later during the Revolutionary War.

Notice that Ben cut his snake into eight pieces, each labeled with the name of one of the colonies. Going from tail to head (south to north) are South Carolina, North Carolina, Virginia, Maryland, Pennsylvania, New Jersey, New York, and New England (comprising Massachusetts, Rhode Island, Connecticut, and New Hampshire). Whoops. That adds up to just twelve colonies. Which one of the original thirteen colonies is missing? Why do you think Ben chose to omit this particular state? Hint: You may need to do a little research.

As "pictures that say a thousand words," political cartoons take aim at newsworthy people or events in a humorous, entertaining way. Yet their main purpose is not so much to amuse as to persuade. An effective political cartoon makes you think about current events, but it also tries to sway your opinion toward the cartoonist's point of view. That's why you can find them in any daily newspaper, but *not* in the comics section. Instead, look on the editorial page—they're usually next to the editorial columns and across from the opinion essays.

You can also find political cartoons on the Internet. A good place to start is www.cagle.com, which is filled with recently published political cartoons on a wide range of controversial topics. Your job is to pick a cartoon—any cartoon that catches your fancy—and write a thoughtful, one-page essay on what you think the cartoonist is trying to tell the reader and how the cartoonist attempts to convey that message. For example, Ben used the image of the snake to emphasize colonial unity during wartime. It may help to read up on your topic before you write your essay, so that you have a fuller context of the event or person about which the cartoonist is commenting.

References

Books and Magazines

* Denotes books and magazines of special interest to middle readers.
† Denotes sources for quotations in this chapter.

* † Adler, David A. *B. Franklin, Printer.* New York: Holiday House, 2001.

* Fleming, Candace. *Ben Franklin's Almanac: Being a True Account of the Good Gentleman's Life.* New York: Atheneum Books for Young Readers, 2003.

Fradin, Dennis Brindell. *Who Was Ben Franklin?* New York: Grosset & Dunlap, 2002.

* † Franklin, Benjamin. *The Autobiography of Benjamin Franklin.* Mineola, NY: Dover Books, 1986.

* Giblin, James Cross. *The Amazing Life of Benjamin Franklin.* New York: Scholastic Press, 2000.

* Harness, Cheryl. *The Remarkable Benjamin Franklin.* Washington, DC: National Geographic Society, 2005.

Isaacson, Walter. *Benjamin Franklin: An American Life.* New York: Simon & Schuster, 2003.

* Morgan, Edmund S., and Sarah Elder Hale, eds. *Appleseeds' Benjamin Franklin.* Peru, IL: Carus, December 2004 issue.

Murphy, Frank. *Ben Franklin and the Magic Squares.* New York: Random House, 2001.

* Noll, Cheryl Kirk. *The Ben Franklin Book of Easy and Incredible Experiments.* New York: John Wiley and Sons, 1995.

Sherrow, Victoria. *Benjamin Franklin.* Minneapolis: Lerner, 2002.

Additional Resources

Web Sites

Benjamin Franklin's Autobiography: www.earlyamerica.com/lives/franklin/index.html. The amazing story of Ben's life written by Ben himself.

Ben Franklin's Pennsylvania Gazette 1728–1800: www.accessible.com. Read editions of Ben's newspapers.

The World of Benjamin Franklin: www.fi.edu/franklin/rotten.html. At this kid-friendly site, visitors may see a short movie called "Glimpses of the Man," a Franklin family tree, a glossary, and much more.

The Electric Ben Franklin: www.ushistory.org/franklin/index.htm. This site includes scholarly articles about Ben, as well as fun activities allowing visitors to tour Declaration Hall, play a game of checkers with Ben, or read grandson Temple's diary.

Places to Visit in Philadelphia

Independence Hall. Visit the Assembly Room, where Ben joined delegates in adopting the Declaration of Independence and framing the U.S. Constitution.

Franklin Court. Located just a few blocks from Independence Hall, the Franklin Court includes an underground museum and three historic houses built by Ben. In one of those houses is the Printing Office and Bindery, where you can see the printing and bookmaking techniques used by Ben and the other colonists.

Franklin Institute Science Museum. This museum houses the largest collection of Franklin memorabilia found anywhere in the world.

Benjamin Franklin Bust. This sixteen-foot-high bust is made from 80,000 copper pennies symbolizing Ben's popular saying, "A penny saved is a penny earned."

Christ Church and its Burial Ground. Although the cemetery is not open to the public, Ben's grave—usually covered in pennies—can be seen through an openwork fence. According to local tradition, tossing a penny on Ben's grave brings good luck.

Videos

Benjamin Franklin: An Extraordinary Life, an Electric Mind. PBS, 2002.

Ben Franklin. A&E Home Video, 2004.

Illustration Credits

In the order photos appear in this chapter: 1. Dr. William J. Ball, Department of Political Science, The College of New Jersey. 2. Dr. William J. Ball. 3. Dr. William J. Ball. 4. Courtesy of the Perry-Castaneda Library, University of Texas at Austin. 5. Dr. William J. Ball. 6. The History Project, University of California at Davis.

Frederick Douglass

1818–1895

Frederick Douglass

If there were just three words to describe Frederick Douglass, they would be "tough as nails." Frederick was born into slavery on a plantation in Maryland. He was taken away from his mother while still just a baby. Later, he was whipped by his owners, forced to work long hours under the blazing hot sun, starved of food, barely clothed, and oftentimes "treated no better than a pig."

Through it all, Frederick dreamed of a better life. "From the time I was very young," he said, "I knew that I would not remain a slave for the whole of my life." Books and newspapers were his ticket out. Not only that, Frederick was convinced that every slave's "pathway from slavery to freedom" was lined with books. Teaching some forty slaves how to read—and dream of a better, freer world—was "the sweetest engagement with which I was ever blessed," he said.

But that is not all Frederick did to free slaves. He was an eloquent speaker who traveled across New England and even as far away as the British Isles, addressing abolitionist meetings on what it was like to be a slave. His words often brought his audiences to tears. As a gifted writer, he started a newspaper called the North Star, *which brought much-needed attention to the horrors of slavery. Moreover, he joined forces with Harriet Tubman in helping slaves escape to freedom in the North by way of the Underground Railroad, even offering his home as a rest stop for runaway slaves.*

By the time of the Civil War, Frederick was one of the most famous black men in America. He became a confidant of President Abraham Lincoln, convincing him to allow African American soldiers to fight in the Union Army. "Liberty won by white men would lose half its luster. ... Better even die free, than to live slaves." After the war, Frederick advocated basic human rights for all Americans.

To learn more, read Escape from Slavery: The Boyhood of Frederick Douglass in His Own Words, *edited and illustrated for young readers by Michael McCurdy. You will better appreciate why Frederick Douglass is regarded not only as an eloquent writer and orator, but as one of the greatest freedom fighters of all time.*

TUCKAHOE, MARYLAND, 1817 or 1818—Frederick Augustus Washington Bailey was born into slavery on a small farm in Maryland. He had a grand name, shortened and sweetened by his mother to "Little Valentine." Because Frederick never knew the actual date he was born, he adopted February 14 (Valentine's Day) as his birthday. Other slave children did the same thing, choosing their own birthday. Frederick explained, "I do not remember to have *ever* met a slave who could tell his own birthday. They seldom come nearer to it than planting-time, harvest-time, cherry-time, spring-time, or fall-time."

Frederick spent his early years near a town called Tuckahoe on Maryland's Eastern Shore. As the story goes, Tuckahoe got its name when a farmer "took a hoe" belonging to another man. The name just stuck. Sadly, Frederick's parents did not. "Of my father I know nothing," Frederick later wrote, other than that he was a white man and perhaps his master. The uncertainty bothered Frederick his entire life.

So, too, did Frederick's "distant" relationship with his mother. Soon after giving birth to Frederick, Harriet Bailey was sent back to work as a field hand ("the most cruel of labors") on a plantation some twelve miles away. Frederick stayed behind and was raised in a small log cabin by his grandparents, whom he later described as "the greatest people in the world to me."

Frederick managed to see his mother only four or five times after their separation, albeit briefly. It's remarkable they managed to see one another at all. To visit Frederick, his mother had to walk the dozen miles at night, after what had already been a long and hard day working in the fields, and then make the return trip to the plantation in time for her morning chores. If she were the tiniest bit late for work, she ran the risk of being whipped by her master with a heavy cowhide or hickory stick.

Frederick was usually in bed when his mother arrived and crawled into bed next to him. Those warm and snuggly hours together were as precious as gold, yet they passed all too quickly. "She would lie down with me, and get me to sleep, but long before I waked she was gone," Frederick wrote. His mother disappeared so quickly he never even got to see her "deep black, glossy complexion" in daylight, and she never got to see the "intelligent smiles of her child."

Harriett died, perhaps from exhaustion, when Frederick was just seven years old. On what turned out to be her last visit, she brought her "Little Valentine" a heart-shaped cake—a gift he would remember the rest of his life. So indifferent were slave owners to the feelings of their slaves, Frederick was not allowed to be with his mother during her illness, at her death, or even during her burial. "She was gone long before I knew anything about it," he sadly recalled.

Despite the painful loss, Frederick fondly remembered his mother for one very special quality. "She was the only one of all the colored people of Tuckahoe who could read. In view of this fact, I am happy to attribute any love of letters I have … to the native genius of my … mother."

TUCKAHOE, MARYLAND (GREAT FARM HOUSE), 1824—Shortly after his mother died, Frederick was put to work on a corn and tobacco plantation called the Great Farm House. "This was my first introduction to the realities of the slave system," he later wrote.

For food, Frederick ate a bland-tasting, coarse cornmeal porridge. "Like so many pigs," he crouched down at a long trough with the other slaves, scooping the porridge with an oyster shell or a piece of tree bark. The strongest and fastest slaves got the most to eat at the trough, but even they rarely filled their bellies. Frederick often felt so hungry that he fought Old Nep, the dog, for scraps and crumbs.

As for clothing, Frederick was given almost nothing to wear. "In the hottest summer and coldest winter I was kept almost naked—no shoes, no stockings, no jacket, no trousers, nothing on but a coarse tow linen shirt reaching only to my knees," he later wrote. If that coarse linen shirt fell apart from wear and tear before the year was over, he went naked.

Frederick was even denied something as simple as a blanket. To keep warm during the cold winter nights, he often crawled headfirst into an empty cornmeal sack. Head in, but feet out. On several occasions his bare feet became frostbitten. "My feet have been so cracked with frost," he noted later, "that the pen with which I am writing might be laid in the gashes."

It didn't take long for Frederick to realize that slaves on the plantation were treated no better than animals. "I had no bed," he wrote. "The pigs in the pen had leaves, and the horses in the stable had straw, but the children had no beds."

One incident in particular drove home the animal-like way slaves were treated. As punishment for being disobedient, Frederick's Aunt Hester was taken into the kitchen, stripped to the waist, hung from a hook by her bound wrists, and whipped until blood streamed down her back. Frederick was so frightened by his aunt's beating that he hid in a closet for hours on end, terrified that he would be next. He wasn't. But he could never escape the memory of that day. "Everybody in the South seemed to want the privilege of whipping somebody else," Frederick painfully recalled many years later.

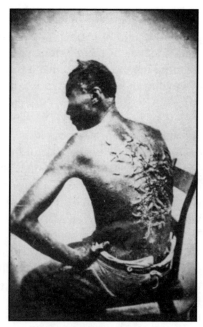

Brutal whipping of a slave

BALTIMORE, MARYLAND (AULD PLANTATION), 1826—As was typical for young slaves, Frederick was soon uprooted and moved to a new home, this time the bustling port of Baltimore, Maryland. His stay marked a turning point in his life. "Going to live in Baltimore," Frederick would later say, "laid the foundation, and opened the gateway, to all my subsequent prosperity."

As soon as the front door opened, Frederick knew he was going to like his new home. He was shown to his own bedroom with a straw bed and plenty of covers, and he sat at a wooden table to eat hearty meals of meat, cornbread, and milk. "I had been treated as a pig on the plantation," Frederick wrote. "In this house I was treated as a child."

Frederick's new mistress was Miss Sophia Auld, "a woman of the kindest heart and finest feelings." He even admitted that he did not think of her so much as a mistress but as "something more akin to a mother." She, in turn, lavished attention on Frederick, reading the Bible to him daily (in her "mellow, loud and sweet" voice) and teaching him the ABC's. Soon he was spelling three and four letter words, and even stringing some of those words into written sentences.

Yet the warm and nurturing relationship forged between teacher and student did not last long. Because Miss Sophia had only recently become a slave owner, she did not realize that it was illegal—that's right, against the law—to teach a slave to read. It was feared at the time that if slaves could read, they would learn about places where they would be free, become dissatisfied with their lot in life, desire their freedom, and eventually escape.

When Miss Sophia's husband, Hugh Auld, finally got wind of what was going on, he insisted that Frederick's reading lessons cease immediately:

> *If you give a nigger an inch, he will take an ell [45 inches]. A nigger should know nothing but to obey his master—to do as he is told to do. Learning would spoil the best nigger in the world. Now if you teach that nigger how to read, there would be no keeping him. It would forever unfit him to be a slave. He would at once become unmanageable, and of no value to his master. As to himself it could do him no good, but a great deal of harm. It would make him discontented and unhappy.*

Miss Sophia not only acquiesced to her husband's order to stop teaching Frederick how to read, she also began to eye Frederick like a hawk to make sure he did not dare to read on his own. Her once "tender heart became stone, and lamblike disposition gave way to one of tiger-like fierceness," Frederick remembered. If he were caught reading a newspaper, Miss Sophia quickly snatched it away from him "with a face made up of fury." If he were alone in a room for too long a time, he was suspected of reading a book and "at once called to give an account of [himself]."

The whole experience left Frederick feeling hurt and confused. He wrote: "Nature made us friends, but slavery had made us enemies. … She had changed, and … I, too, had changed. We were both victims to the same overshadowing evil, she as mistress, I as slave."

From *Readers and Leaders* by Susan Steffensen Romaine. Westport, CT: Libraries Unlimited.
Copyright © 2007 Libraries Unlimited.

Yet Frederick would not remain a victim of slavery for long. Just as Miss Sophia was dead set on preventing him from obtaining an education, he became more determined than ever to read. If knowledge made a slave unfit, Frederick reasoned, then knowledge was precisely what he most desired. "Mistress, in teaching me the alphabet, had given me the inch, and no precaution could prevent me from taking the ell [45 inches]," Frederick later wrote in his autobiography. There would be no turning back now.

BALTIMORE, MARYLAND, 1826—There were many obstacles in Frederick's path to reading. He had no pencils, pens, or paper. He had no books, other than an old Webster's spelling book with a worn cover and tattered pages. He didn't even have a mother, father, or teacher to help him with his lessons. Still, he "set out with high hope, and a fixed purpose, at whatever cost of trouble" to read—for he now believed that books and education were his ticket to freedom.

Frederick found his classroom on the streets. Here's how: one of Frederick's many responsibilities was to run errands for Miss Sophia. Before setting off from home, he always packed his *Webster's Spelling Book* and tucked in a loaf of bread ("enough of which was always in the house, and to which I was always welcome"). That way, once he finished his errands, he would cut a deal with "the hungry little urchins"—the poor white kids from the streets of Baltimore. Frederick offered his bread to the street urchins; in return, they taught him how to read and to acquire "the more valuable bread of knowledge." For this most precious of gifts, Frederick always "felt the strongest attachment to those little Baltimore boys."

To learn to write, Frederick was equally clever. While working in a shipyard, he carefully studied the initials the carpenters scrawled on pieces of lumber to designate their use. (An "L" for the larboard side, "S.F." for starboard side forward, "L.A." for larboard aft, "S.A." for starboard aft, and so forth.) Once he memorized a certain letter, he would proudly write it in chalk on a fence board and say to his street friends, "Let's see you beat that!" Rising to the challenge, his friends would then write various other letters which Frederick again quickly memorized. "During this time," he later recalled, "my copy-book was the board fence, brick wall, and pavement; my pen and ink was a lump of chalk."

Whether it was bartering or trickery, Frederick's plan to educate himself worked. "I learned to read and write in the only way possible for a slave," Frederick wrote. "I stole the knowledge." His ability to read and write soon proved to be his most powerful weapon in his lifelong fight against slavery and prejudice.

* * *

In between reading and writing lessons, thirteen-year-old Frederick talked to his white friends about his yearning to escape slavery. "I am a slave for life," he told them. "Have not I as good a right to be free as you have?"

The answer came to him one day when a friend opened a book and suddenly started reading aloud. Called *The Columbian Orator*, it was filled with great speeches Frederick had never heard before, and it opened up new worlds he never even knew existed. He listened intently to the eloquent words of Roman statesmen Cato and Cicero. He lapped up William Pitt's speech to the British Parliament and George Washington's farewell address to his troops after the American Revolution. He was moved by Daniel O'Connell's plea for the emancipation, or freeing, of oppressed Catholics in Ireland.

But to Frederick's ears, the most stirring words from *The Columbian Orator* came in an exchange between a slave and his master. "Prove that slavery is wrong," said the master. "Then I will set you free." The slave argued that God intended for all men to be equal and, therefore, God would not have created some men to be masters and some to be slaves. So it must be that slavery was *not* God's will; it was immoral. The slave's argument was so convincing that his master finally set him free.

Eager to purchase his own copy of *The Columbian Orator*, Frederick got a job as a shoeshine boy. As soon as he had saved up fifty cents, he made a beeline to the nearest Baltimore bookstore. It was the first book he ever owned, and it quickly became his most prized possession. He slipped it into his pocket when visiting the wharfs in Baltimore, hiding among the ships and cargo so he could read for hours at a time without fear of being caught. The book deeply moved Frederick, inspiring him to read dozens more books

From *Readers and Leaders* by Susan Steffensen Romaine. Westport, CT: Libraries Unlimited.

about abolitionists—men and women, black and white, young and old—fighting to end slavery in the United States.

Just as Hugh Auld had predicted, the more Frederick read, the more he resented slavery and longed to be free. Not only that, he wished *all* his brethren were literate so that they, too, could read about the injustices of slavery described in *The Columbian Orator* and dare to seek their freedom. As a first step, Frederick secretly started a Sunday school devoted "to teaching these my loved fellow-slaves how to read." Using just a few old spelling books and Bibles, he instructed "over forty scholars … ardently desiring to learn." It was a labor of love. "The work of instructing my dear fellow-slaves was the sweetest engagement with which I was ever blessed," Frederick later wrote.

NEW YORK CITY, NEW YORK, 1838—Frederick was by now a tall, strapping, twenty-year-old man, wanting nothing more in life than to be free. "For my part, I had become altogether too big for my chains," he wrote. His new master, Thomas Auld, quoted from the Bible as he cruelly beat his slaves and tried to "break" their rebellious spirit. Frederick yearned to be free of that hypocrisy. He yearned to be free of brutal whippings. Free of hunger pains. Free of cold winter nights. Free of long days toiling in the hot sun. Free to come and go as he pleased. Free to speak his mind.

To be truly free, Frederick knew he must flee to the North where there was no slavery. This was by no means an easy task. For just as Frederick read stories about those lucky enough to escape slavery, he read many more stories about those who were caught and returned to their masters for rewards, sold to other slave owners, or even killed. "It was life and death with me," Frederick wrote of his planned escape.

Slave sale in Easton, Maryland.

For his escape, Frederick hoped to take advantage of "the kind feeling that prevailed in Baltimore … towards those who go down to the sea in ships." He disguised himself as a sailor, donning a red shirt, a handkerchief around his neck, and a flat-topped, broad-brimmed sailor's hat on his head. He even talked like a sailor. "My knowledge of ships and sailors' talk came much to my assistance," he wrote, "for I knew a ship from stem to stem, and from keelson to crosstrees, and could talk sailor like an *old salt*."

Riding three trains, three ferries, and a steamboat, Frederick finally reached New York City and freedom. It was as if he had escaped a den of hungry lions. "Dreams of my childhood and the purposes of my manhood were now fulfilled," Frederick remembered. "A free state around me, and a free state under my feet! What a moment was this to me!" He would never call another man master again.

From *Readers and Leaders* by Susan Steffensen Romaine. Westport, CT: Libraries Unlimited.
Copyright © 2007 Libraries Unlimited.

Once settled, Frederick proposed marriage to Anna Murray, a free African American woman working as a housekeeper in Baltimore. She accepted and agreed to join him in the North.

NEW BEDFORD, MASSACHUSETTS, 1838—From New York, Frederick and Anna moved to New Bedford, Massachusetts, a seaport known for its many whaling ships and its strong antislavery sentiment. "Here, people are far wealthier than any plantation owner—they are rich with freedom," said Frederick.

To escape slave catchers on the lookout for runaways, Frederick Augustus Washington Bailey's first order of business was to change his last name. A friend suggested Douglas, after a brave and heroic Scottish chieftain in Sir Walter Scott's poem "Lady of the Lake." Adding an *s* to make the name more unique, Frederick Douglass it was. "A new name for a new life," he exclaimed.

In New Bedford, Frederick worked as a stevedore, loading and unloading ship cargoes. He also chopped wood, shoveled coal, dug cellars, moved rubbish, and swept chimneys. It was backbreaking work for meager pay, but Frederick didn't mind. For the first time in his life he didn't have to "pour the reward of my toil into the purse of my master." He could keep all his wages for his growing family.

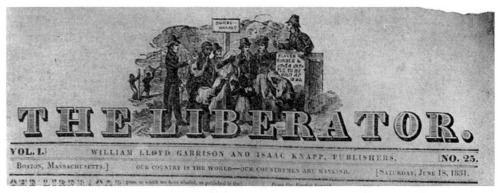

The Liberator's masthead.

During his free time, Frederick read William Lloyd Garrison's newspaper, *The Liberator*. Garrison was the best-known voice against slavery at the time, arguing that blacks were citizens of this nation and should be granted the exact same rights as all other Americans. "The paper came," said Frederick, "and I read it from week to week with such feelings as it would be quite idle for me to attempt to describe. The paper became my meat and my drink. My soul was set all on fire. Its sympathy for my brethren in bonds—its scathing denunciations of slaveholders—its faithful exposures of slavery—and its powerful attacks upon the upholders of the institution—sent a thrill of joy through my soul, such as I had never felt before."

Frederick was so moved by his readings of *The Liberator,* he began speaking out against slavery, mob violence, and lynching in the South ("where every breeze was tainted and freighted with Negro blood"). He also challenged the many forms of segregation he witnessed in the North. Due to Jim Crow laws, Frederick could not sit next to whites in church pews, nor could he enter many stores and restaurants owned by whites. On ships he had to remain on deck, even in stormy weather, or ride below with the baggage. On trains he could only ride in special cars for blacks, which were often crowded and smelly. "Dogs and monkeys can ride first class," one of Frederick's friends said bitterly. "But not Frederick Douglass."

With his flashing dark eyes, white pressed shirts, broad shoulders, mass of black hair, six-foot-two-inch frame, and biting tongue, Frederick commanded lots of attention. "As a speaker, he has few equals," proclaimed the Concord, Massachusetts, newspaper. In fact, he spoke so eloquently that some people began to wonder if he spoke *too* well. How could a slave know so many fine and fancy words? Was he just making up his stories? Was he some kind of fraud? Rumors spread. Audiences whispered that it just didn't seem possible for a runaway slave with no formal schooling to sound so articulate.

To put all doubts to rest, Frederick decided to write the story of his life as a slave, which he titled *The Narrative of the Life of Frederick Douglass, An American Slave.* In it, he revealed all: who he was, whose slave he had been, how he had suffered, his education, his escape—everything. Even though such a detailed book might lead to his capture and return to slavery, Frederick wrote it anyway. Much like Harriet Beecher Stowe's *Uncle Tom's Cabin,* it proved to be a credible and powerful story, enabling many Americans for the first time to come to grips with the cruelty of slavery. "If it does not open the eyes of this people," one reviewer wrote, "they must be petrified into eternal sleep."

Harriet Beecher Stowe

ROCHESTER, NEW YORK, 1846—After a two-year stay in Great Britain, escaping slave catchers while also drumming up support for the American abolitionist cause, Frederick was now widely regarded as "liberty's voice." He moved his family to upstate New York, where he began publishing his own weekly newspaper, the *North Star.* The paper got its name because slaves escaping at night were told: "Just follow that old North Star in the sky. It will lead you to freedom." Frederick hoped the *North Star* would lead thousands of slaves to freedom through its inspiring speeches, articles, poems, and essays by black writers. On the masthead appeared the motto, "Right is of no sex—Truth is of no color—God is the father of us all, and we are all Brethren."

During his years as publisher of the *North Star,* Frederick broadened his agenda from freeing slaves to liberating *all* oppressed Americans. He joined ranks with Susan B. Anthony and pushed for women's suffrage, or the right to vote. He exposed the horrific poverty in the South. He spoke out against children working long hours in dark and dirty factories. During the Civil War, Frederick convinced President Lincoln to allow black soldiers to fight in the Union Army and then recruited thousands of soldiers (including two of his own sons) to join the cause.

"I am not only an American slave," said Frederick, "but a man, and as such, am bound to use my powers for the welfare of the whole human brotherhood."

President Abraham Lincoln

From *Readers and Leaders* by Susan Steffensen Romaine. Westport, CT: Libraries Unlimited.
Copyright © 2007 Libraries Unlimited.

Publishing the *North Star* was a family affair. The office was one room of the Douglass home in Rochester. While Frederick edited stories submitted by black writers, his five children helped set the letters for the printing press and folded and delivered the newspapers. Anna, who never learned to read, helped out by cooking a special meal to celebrate each new issue of the paper.

Although the *North Star* was often plagued with financial troubles, Frederick never regretted his decision to become its publisher. "I have come to think that it was the best school possible for me," he later wrote. "It obliged me to think and read, it taught me to express my thoughts clearly and was perhaps better than any other course I could have adopted."

WASHINGTON, DC, 1872—After the Civil War, Frederick moved to a fifteen-acre estate overlooking Washington, DC. Surrounded by cedar trees, he named his estate Cedar Hill. Ironically, it had once been the homestead of Confederate General Robert E. Lee. Frederick continued to stay active in both social and political causes, but for the first time he also relaxed with his favorite hobbies. His home had a spacious library where he read the plays of William Shakespeare and the poems of Lord Byron and John Greenleaf Whittier. It also had a music room where he played his violin from time to time. "No man can be an enemy of mine who loves the violin," Frederick once said.

It was in Cedar Hill that Frederick died of a heart attack at age seventy-seven. Fittingly, he had just returned home from a women's suffrage meeting, fighting for a cause that he cared about deeply, almost until his very last breath.

* * *

Frederick once told a group of African American students from a school in Talbot County, Maryland, "What was possible for me is possible for you. Do not think because you are colored you cannot accomplish anything. Strive earnestly to add to your knowledge. So long as you remain in ignorance, so long will you fail to command the respect of your fellow men."

It is hard to imagine anyone who worked harder than Frederick to overcome so many obstacles in life. As a young boy, he might easily have become one more among the millions of slaves with little chance for a decent life. Instead, by reading books, he dreamed of first becoming a free man and then of liberating all his brethren. Through newspapers, he envisioned a world where men and women were judged not so much by the color of their skin but by the content of their character, in the words of Martin Luther King. Through books, he learned that words—not arms—were the greatest weapon against slavery and prejudice, laying the very foundation for the civil rights movement that would take shape under Martin Luther King a half century later. "One man's skin can be black and another man's skin can be white," Frederick once said, "but under the skin we are all the same." Amen.

Going the Extra Mile:
Extension Activities for Frederick Douglass

I. Richard Wright

Just a few years after Frederick Douglass died, the highly acclaimed African American writer Richard Wright was born near Natchez, Mississippi. Their lives paralleled each other in many ways, most notably in their fierce determination to get their hands on books. As a young boy, Wright was not allowed to borrow books from public libraries in the segregated South simply because of the color of his skin. Yet he did not let that stop him. When he began working for an optical company as a teenager, he borrowed a library card from a white coworker to check out H. L. Mencken's *Prejudices* and *A Book of Prefaces*, Sinclair Lewis's *Main Street*, and Theodore Dreiser's *Jennie Gerhardt* and *Sister Carrie*. In Wright's own words, these books were "like a drug, a dope … that created moods in which I lived for days." They later inspired him to write and ultimately become an internationally best-selling author.

Wright's moving account of borrowing a library card from a coworker to open his world to books is described in his autobiography, *Black Boy*. Read it. (It comprises just one chapter near the end of Part One: Southern Night). Then write an essay comparing and contrasting the obstacles Richard Wright and Frederick Douglass overcame simply to read. What were the common threads in their experiences? In what fundamental ways did their experiences differ?

II. Underground Railroad

The Underground Railroad is a confusing name. It was not an actual railroad, nor was it literally underground. It refers to the many routes that slaves traveled as they attempted to escape from southern states, where slavery was legal, to northern states and Canada where slaves would be free. To see a map of some of the more popular escape routes, go to the National Geographic's Underground Railroad Web site at www.nationalgeographic.com/railroad/index.html and select "Routes to Freedom" from the drop-down menu.

Look carefully at the map and notice the location of mountains and rivers. What elements of nature would the runaway slaves have been most concerned about? Now think about other dangers the runaways faced and ways they may have overcome those obstacles. Jot them down on a sheet of a paper. You can add to your list by referring back to the National Geographic Web site and selecting "The Journey" and "Routes to Freedom" and "For Kids" from the drop-down menu.

Now that you have researched the pros and cons of riding the Underground Railroad, one question remains. What would you have done? Would you have risked your life by becoming a passenger aboard the Underground Railroad, or played it safe by remaining a slave? Write a one-page essay in which you support your answer with some of the facts and figures gleaned from the National Geographic Web site.

III. Carrying on Frederick Douglass's Legacy

Martin Luther King at Civil Rights March in Washington, D.C.

While studying to become a minister, Martin Luther King attended a lecture about Mahatma Gandhi and his campaign of nonviolent civil disobedience used against British rule in India. King was deeply moved by Gandhi's life, his ideals, and mostly his words. "Through our pain we will make them see their injustice," Gandhi had reportedly told throngs of oppressed Indians living under harsh British rule. As King listened to the lecture, he wondered if Gandhi's message was just as relevant for the millions of blacks living in the United States who were also being denied the rights of full citizenship.

So began Martin Luther King's civil rights movement in the United States. Through student sit-ins, economic boycotts, the ballot box, and various other methods, King and his Southern Christian Leadership Council adopted the motto, "Not one hair of one head of one person should be harmed."

The very first student sit-in occurred in Greensboro, North Carolina, in 1960. Four African American college students sat down at a whites-only lunch counter in a local Woolworth's and ordered coffee. They were denied service for no reason other than the color of their skin. In protest, the students refused to leave their seats at the lunch counter until the store closed at 5 PM. Within days, hundreds of college students joined in sit-ins at Woolworth's and other stores in Greensboro; in two months, the sit-in demonstrations had spread to 54 cities in nine states. (For more background information, read "Greensboro Sit-ins: Launch of a Civil Rights Movement" at www.sitins.com/index.shtml.)

The sit-ins generated strong feelings on both sides of the issue. Many local townspeople argued that the four African American students should be forcibly removed from the lunch counter for threatening public safety. Civil rights leaders such as Martin Luther King and Thurgood Marshall "countered" that the sit-ins were protected under the First Amendment's right to assembly.

To understand the legal issues more fully, read "First Principles" found at http://www. freedomforum.org/packages/first/curricula/educationforfreedom/FirstPrinciples.htm. It explains in practical, everyday terms just what the First Amendment to the Constitution means. Then bring it all closer to home by writing a School Bill of Rights, which lays out your right to assemble (or to gather in groups for peaceful and lawful purposes) in your school and on its grounds. Under what circumstances should this right always be recognized by your principal? Under what conditions could it be denied? Be as specific as possible.

References

Books and Magazines

Denotes books and magazines of special interest to middle readers.

†*Denotes sources for quotations in this chapter.*

* † Douglass, Frederick. *Narrative of the Life of Frederick Douglass: An American Slave Written by Himself.* New York: Oxford University Press, 1960.

* † McCurdy, Michael. *Escape from Slavery: The Boyhood of Frederick Douglass in His Own Words.* New York: Alfred A. Knopf, 1994.

McKissack, Patricia and Frederick. *Frederick Douglass: The Black Lion.* Chicago: Childrens Press, 1987.

* † Miller, Douglas T. *Frederick Douglass and the Fight for Freedom.* New York: Facts on File Publications, 1988.

* † Russell, Sharman Apt. *Frederick Douglass, Abolitionist Editor.* New York: Chelsea House Publishers, 1988.

* † Schraff, Anne. *Frederick Douglass Speaking Out against Slavery.* Berkeley Heights, NJ: Enslow, 2002.

Weidt, Maryann N., *Voice of Freedom: A Story about Frederick Douglass.* Minneapolis: Carolrhoda Books, 2001.

* Yoder, Carolyn P., ed. *Cobblestone's Frederick Douglass: Fighter for Freedom.* Peterborough, New Hampshire: Cobblestone, February 1989 issue.

Additional Resources

Web Sites

Frederick Douglass National Historic Site: www.nps.gov/frdo/freddoug.html. A visual tour of Cedar Hill and links to related sites.

Western New York Suffragists: Frederick Douglass: winningthevote.org/FDouglass.html. A short biography of Frederick Douglass with links to people and events in his life.

Index of Frederick Douglass Historic Documents: www.usc.edu/isd/archives/ethnicstudies/ historicdocs/Douglass/. Articles written by Frederick Douglass as well as other famous African Americans.

Places to Visit

Cedar Hill in Washington, D.C. Frederick's home is now a National Historic Site and open to the public. Tours include the one-room study behind the house where Frederick liked to read and think in peace.

Museum of Afro American History in Boston, Massachusetts. See the meeting house where the abolitionist movement began and Frederick passionately spoke out against slavery.

Museum of African American History in Detroit, Michigan. Learn about the Underground Railroad and its role in helping thousands of slaves escape slavery in the South and find freedom in the North.

Videos

Biography—Frederick Douglass. A&E Home Video, 2005.

Underground Railroad. A&E Home Video, 2002.

Illustration Credits

In the order photos appear in this chapter: 1. Courtesy of the Perry-Castaneda Library, University of Texas at Austin. 2. Dr. William J. Ball, Department of Political Science, The College of New Jersey. 3. Dr. William J. Ball. 4. Dr. William J. Ball. 5. Dr. William J. Ball. 6. Wikimedia Commons. 7. Dr. William J. Ball.

Emily Dickinson

1830–1886

Emily Dickinson

Some say friends are our greatest treasure. They double our joys and halve our sorrows. The math is as simple as that.

Every once in a while, though, people come along who are perfectly content without the company of friends. Known as recluses, they are happiest just "going it alone." One of America's foremost poets, Emily Dickinson, was one such recluse. For the last twenty years of her life, Emily stayed holed up in her house or its surrounding gardens, with just her parents and sister as companions. "You may laugh at the idea that I cannot be happy when away from home," she wrote to a friend, "but you must remember that I have a very dear home." In that home she devoted herself to the one thing that never made her feel lonely: books.

Reading gave Emily a strong, emotional tie to the world around her—a connection she was unable to achieve through her interactions with people. She often cited books as the best company of all, referring to them as "Kinsmen [or friends] of the Shelf." Through them, she visited foreign lands, traveled in time, stayed informed of current events and new trends in literature, and experienced all the swings of human emotion that most of us get through our relationships with friends and family.

But it was not enough for Emily simply to read the works of other writers. She wanted to write, too, drawing inspiration from her daily reading of the Bible, classical myths, Webster's Dictionary, *church hymns, classical and popular literature, newspapers and magazines, and even science textbooks. Her lifework of some 1,775 poems, which she collectively called "My letter to the World, That never wrote to Me," can be found in* The Complete Poems of Emily Dickinson, *edited by Thomas H. Johnson. By reading it, you will better appreciate Emily's vivid and colorful imagination, allowing her to write intimately about places she had never been and things she had never seen.*

I never saw a moor,
I never saw the sea,
Yet know I how the heather looks,
And what a wave must be.

From *Readers and Leaders* by Susan Steffensen Romaine. Westport, CT: Libraries Unlimited.
Copyright © 2007 Libraries Unlimited.

Emily Dickinson was born in a red brick house sitting behind a high evergreen hedge in the little college town of Amherst, Massachusetts. Known as The Homestead, the house was surrounded by a vegetable garden as well as row after row of apple, pear, cherry, and peach trees. A nearby greenhouse produced fresh flowers all year long. While tending to the hollyhocks and roses, Emily first discovered her love of nature—a passion that would later become a common theme in her poetry.

The Homestead was built by Emily's grandfather, Samuel Fowler Dickinson, who also founded Amherst College. Suffice it to say, the Dickinsons were a prominent family in their community. Emily would later feel so rooted to her hometown that she used the penname, "Amherst," when she signed many of her letters.

Outside of its college, Amherst was a sleepy town. There were a few general stores, a Congregational Church, and a bookstore that carried only those books the townspeople considered to be "wholesome reading." The most frequently read book in the Dickinson household was the Bible. Every morning and evening, Emily's father read to the family from the Bible and then led them in prayer. He was a very proper and religious man, so well known around town that many people called him "Squire" Dickinson.

By contrast, Emily's mother was a cold, distant figure. Suffering from depression, she was often bedridden and displayed little affection for Emily, her older brother, Austin, or her younger sister, Lavinia. "I never had a mother," Emily once said. "I suppose a mother is one to whom you hurry when you are troubled."

At age four, Emily eagerly started school. She quickly learned to read and write, using a textbook called the *New England Primer*. The book was filled with prayers and religious rhymes to inspire its young readers to lead a good life in hopes of going to heaven one day. Emily read and memorized many of the prayers and rhymes, which decades later showed up in her poetry.

I never spoke with God,
Nor visited in heaven;
Yet certain am I of the spot
As if the chart were given.

Emily was encouraged to not only attend the finest schools but to excel in her studies. Her father was a firm believer that girls should be educated just as well as boys, even though, at the time, there were few career opportunities for women outside of the home. So it was that nine-year-old Emily was enrolled at Amherst Academy, a rigorous all-girls school. She fared well in all her courses, but Emily's teachers were most impressed with her writing skills. "Her compositions were unlike anything ever heard and always produced a sensation," her brother recalled. "Her imagination sparkled and she gave it free rein."

To read, Emily faced some steep obstacles. The Congregational Church preached that reading books (other than the Bible) was a bad influence on the minds of young people, a view to which Emily's father subscribed. "He buys me many Books—but begs me not to read them—because he fears they joggle the mind," Emily wrote in a letter to a friend.

To avoid the wrath of the Church and her father, Emily did most of her reading in private. She hid Henry Wadsworth Longfellow's popular romantic novel, *Kavanagh*, under a piano cover where it was unlikely to be discovered. Other books of fiction she hid in the bushes near her front door or the woods outside her house.

Emily and her brother, Austin, also sneaked books of all kinds into their bedroom for what they called "reading feasts." As friends learned of their dealings, they, too, joined in and together formed a Shakespeare Club. Books were exchanged almost like baseball cards, while plots and characters were dissected and analyzed.

Henry Wadsworth Longfellow

From *Readers and Leaders* by Susan Steffensen Romaine. Westport, CT: Libraries Unlimited.
Copyright © 2007 Libraries Unlimited.

William Shakespeare

The Shakespeare Club marked the beginning of Emily's lifelong love of words. She enjoyed trying to solve riddles and create puns or other plays on words. As a hobby, she started reading *Webster's Dictionary,* savoring the definitions as if they were sweets. This passion showed up in some of her later poems as extended play on words.

Hope is the thing with feathers
That perches in the soul
And sings the tune without the words,
And never stops at all.

Intensely shy, Emily left home at age sixteen to attend the Mount Holyoke Female Seminary (today known as Mount Holyoke College) in South Hadley, Massachusetts. It was a long and difficult transition. For starters, Emily was uneasy with the seminary's mission to train women to go out into the world and spread Christianity. By this time Emily was moving in the completely opposite direction, refusing to attend church services or even call herself a Christian. "Christ is calling everyone here, all my companions have answered … and I am standing alone in rebellion." As a rebel, she felt the sting of classmates who called her a "no hoper" and for the first time began to sense her "otherness."

To make matters worse, Emily, who was keenly interested in world events, felt cut off from life outside Mount Holyoke's campus. Her frustrations surfaced in a letter to her brother, Austin: "Won't you please tell me … who the candidate for President is? I have been trying to find out ever since I came here & have not yet succeeded. I don't know anything more about affairs in the world, than if I was in a trance."

Alfred, Lord Tennyson

Emily's homesickness soon turned into another kind of sickness, a hacking cough. She returned home to convalesce, cuddling up in bed for weeks with her books. She had a reading feast with "Evangeline" (a poem by Henry Wadsworth Longfellow), *The Princess* (by Alfred, Lord Tennyson), *The Maiden Aunt* (by Marcella Bute Smedley), *The Epicurean* (by Thomas Moore), and the *Twins and Heart* (by Tupper). She also poured over the fifteen or so periodicals delivered to the Dickinson home, including the three most important magazines of the period—the *Atlantic Monthly*, *Harper's Monthly Magazine*, and *Scribner's Monthly Magazine*.

There is no Frigate like a Book
To take us lands away
Nor any Coursers like a Page
Of prancing Poetry.

Despite her long illness Emily was happy to be home again, surrounded by her family and books—so happy that she quit Mount Holyoke after just one year and never returned. It was a turning point in her life, for Emily rarely left her hometown of Amherst again. With the exception of a trip to Washington, D.C. (where her father was serving as a U.S. congressman), a trip to Philadelphia (where she met her "dearest earthly friend" and perhaps the one true love of her life, a Presbyterian preacher), and several trips to Boston (to see a doctor about eye problems), she remained at her family home or in its surrounding gardens for the rest of her life. "I do not cross my father's ground for any house or town," she admitted.

Emily Dickinson at age 20

As a homebody, Emily became known around town as "the Queen Recluse" and "The Hermit," and, because she never married, "the Nun of Amherst." More and more, she preferred the peace and solitude of her bedroom, or the birds and bees and flowers of her garden, to visits with family and friends. On the few occasions when she felt like company, she talked to guests from behind a partially opened door or shouted to them from her upstairs bedroom.

> Even though Emily's best friend and sister-in-law, Susan Gilbert, lived right next door, she didn't visit her for years at a time. Instead, Emily sent servants to the house just "a hedge away" with handwritten letters addressed to "Sister Sue," and poems of friendship for her only niece and two nephews.

As another sign of her quirky nature, Emily began to shun clothes with any hint of color and opted instead to wear only lily white dresses. Oddly enough, she wore her trademark white dresses even while tending to her daily chores such as washing clothes, making beds, scrubbing floors, and kneading dough. She soon developed a passion for baking. "She makes all the bread, for her father only likes hers," a friend once commented.

Her specialty was gingerbread, which she often shared with the children in her neighborhood. From an upstairs window, hidden behind a curtain, this "woman in white" would gently lower a basket filled with warm gingerbread to the children standing below. (See recipe for Emily's *Gingerbread in a Basket* in Extension Activities.) Buried beneath the bread, the children often found odd poems Emily had scribbled on scraps of paper:

I'm Nobody! Who are you?
Are you—Nobody—Too?
Then there's a pair of us!
Don't tell us! They'd advertise us—you know!

From *Readers and Leaders* by Susan Steffensen Romaine. Westport, CT: Libraries Unlimited.
Copyright © 2007 Libraries Unlimited.

By her early thirties, Emily was as prolific as ever. She closeted herself in her sparsely decorated bedroom for days at a time, jotting down notes and verses on all kinds of scrap paper—the back side of a recipe or used envelope, in the margin of a newspaper, on a grocery list or a candy wrapper.

In large and loopy handwriting, Emily labored over each and every poem, marking through words and replacing them with better ones, rearranging lines, and changing punctuation. She kept a dictionary nearby so she could find a word that would say *exactly* what she wanted to convey, and she always strived to use as few words as possible. It was painstaking work. Yet if there was one thing Emily knew for sure, it was what a good poem should do. "If it makes my whole body so cold no fire can ever warm me, I know that is poetry. If I feel physically as if the top of my head were taken off, I know that is poetry."

Emily wrote about people, flowers, trees, birds, butterflies, thunderstorms, sunrises and sunsets, the passage of time—all ordinary things. But she had such a vivid imagination that she seemed to get inside these things and look at them in a whole new way. That is to say, she "dwelled in Possibility." A simple walk along a path with her dog, Carlo, became a visit to the sea. The month of March was a long-awaited visit with a friend. The sun did not merely rise in her poems; it "rose a ribbon at a time." Miraculously, the moon could slide down a chair or show "a chin of gold."

With Emily's imagination, a sunset wasn't just the pretty colors brightening the sky. It was a woman sweeping with a broom, each stroke leaving behind bright and colorful straws. In her poems, hills could untie bonnets. Lightning had a yellow beak and ugly blue claws. A maple tree wore a vibrant scarf. Birds didn't just fly; they unrolled their feathers and rowed home.

To fuel her imagination and gather fresh ideas for her poetry, Emily read and read. Her nose was in a book almost every spare moment, and she carefully marked passages that held special meaning to her. She preferred to read the fiction of Charles Dickens, Nathaniel Hawthorne, George Eliot (whose portrait hung in her bedroom), and the Bronte sisters (especially Charlotte's *Jane Eyre*). But none of these writers could compare in her opinion to the English playwright William Shakespeare. As Emily explained, "I flew to the shelves and devoured the luscious passages. I thought I should tear the [pages] out as I turned them, then I settled down to a willingness for all the rest to go but William Shakespeare."

Emily also read verse after verse of poetry. Among her favorite poets were John Keats, Robert Browning, John Ruskin, Robert Burns, and Henry Wadsworth Longfellow. But it was the poetess Elizabeth Barrett Browning, whose portrait also hung in her bedroom, who stood out from the pack. Emily never tired of reading Barrett Browning's poetry and always felt a special bond with one of her characters, Aurora Leigh. Like Emily, Aurora set her sights on becoming a serious poet instead of following the more conventional path of marriage. Both believed that marriage would only tie them down at a time when they wanted to be free of any encumbrances to pursue their writing.

For a brief period, Emily tried to get some of her poetry published. She read an article in the *Atlantic Monthly* by Thomas Wentworth Higginson, claiming that "every editor is always hungering and thirsting" for new literature. Perhaps he would be interested in hers.

Some weeks later Higginson opened an envelope where he found four poems and a letter with "handwriting so peculiar that it seemed as if the writer might have taken her first lessons by studying the famous fossil bird tracks in the museum of that college town." The letter began with this timid request: "Mr. Higginson, Are you too deeply occupied to say if my verse is alive?"

Elizabeth Barrett Browning

Sadly, Higginson did not recognize the true genius behind Emily's words. Instead, he considered the verses of "my partially cracked poetess at Amherst" stilted, lacking the flowery language most readers preferred at the time. She broke too many "rules" in order to play with an idea in a different way, he thought. She used too many dashes—way too many dashes—in her verse. For some odd reason, she also tended to capitalize Nouns smack in the middle of a line. And to Higginson's great dismay, she never even bothered to title her poems.

Then there was the unusual rhythm, or meter, in her poetry. It was very much like ordinary speech, or the hymns Emily sang in church. If you clapped the rhythm, the first clap was soft or weak, the second loud or strong—similar to the beat in the "Battle Hymn of the Republic." See for yourself by singing this poem to the tune of the "Battle Hymn" (Mine eyes have seen the glory of the coming of the Lord/He is trampling out the vintage where the grapes of wrath are stored).

> *The moon was but a chin of gold*
> *A night or two ago.*
> *And now she turns her perfect face*
> *Upon the world below.*

Some of Emily's other songs could be sung to the tunes of "The Yellow Rose of Texas" or the theme song to "Gilligan's Island," demonstrating the intimate connection between her poetry and music.

Headstrong, Emily refused to make even the slightest changes to her poetry to please her critics. So hundreds of her poems sat in a desk drawer in her bedroom, known only to her. As time passed, fewer and fewer people were aware that Emily even wrote poetry. Of course, her family knew that in between gardening, baking, practicing the piano, letter writing, and caring for her ailing mother, Emily often sat at a small desk beside her bedroom window and wrote poetry. In addition, a few of her closest "friends" knew of her writing ability, because she often included poems of endearment in her birthday greetings and valentine cards. And readers of the *Springfield Republican* knew that she had published seven or eight poems in their newspaper. But for the most part, Emily was better known in her hometown of Amherst for her homemade gingerbread and chocolate caramels than for her poetry.

* * *

At the youthful age of fifty-five, bedridden and dying from Bright's disease, Emily wrote her last note to her two young cousins. It read simply: "Little Cousins, Called Back." Just as she had requested, she was buried in a white casket, wearing a lily white dress. Inscribed on her tombstone were the words, "E.D. Called Back."

Shortly after her death her sister, Vinnie, was sorting through Emily's possessions in her bedroom. There, she discovered a locked box tucked away in the bottom drawer of a bureau. When she opened it, Vinnie could hardly believe her eyes. In it were 1,775 of Emily's previously unseen poems. Many of the poems were neatly written in ink and tied together with needle and thread into forty little bundles, which Emily had referred to as her "fascicles."

Once she read through Emily's lifework, Vinnie knew immediately that the "fascicles" must be shared with the world. So began Vinnie's lifework: to publish Emily's poetry. With tireless determination, she succeeded. The first slender volume of Emily's poetry was published four years after her death. The publication of two more volumes of poetry and a large collection of her letters followed. By the time all of her poems were published seven decades later in *The Complete Poems of Emily Dickinson*, this Belle of Amherst was widely regarded as one of America's premier writers.

In a way, it seems so tragic that Emily died before her poetic gift was fully appreciated and her greatness came to light. But in another way, that's exactly how Emily would have wanted it. She did not write to acquire fame or fortune. Simply seeing the sun rise or the moon glow or the colors of the seasons change was much more gratifying. To Emily, the ability to marvel at the beauty in everything—even the most ordinary of life's occurrences—was the greatest reward of all.

From *Readers and Leaders* by Susan Steffensen Romaine. Westport, CT: Libraries Unlimited.
Copyright © 2007 Libraries Unlimited.

If I can stop one heart from breaking,
I shall not live in vain;
If I can ease one life the aching,
Or cool one pain,
Or help one fainting robin
Unto his nest again,
I shall not live in vain

"People say a word dies when it is written in pen," Emily once wrote, "but for me that word's life is just about to begin." True to her word, Emily's poems live on—and on—and on.

Going the Extra Mile:
Extension Activities for Emily Dickinson

I. Baking Gingerbread

Emily took great pride in her baking skills. She once entered her favorite Rye and Indian bread in a competition at a local fair, taking second place. She bragged to friends that her father refused to eat bread baked by anyone else but her. Yet her greatest satisfaction in baking came from "exchanging affections," sending gifts of bread and candy—along with notes, poems, and flowers—to friends and relatives. It gave her a sense of intimacy with people that she otherwise rarely experienced in her life. Try "exchanging affections" yourself, using Emily's Gingerbread in a Basket recipe for part of the gift-giving.

Emily's Gingerbread in a Basket

(Adapted from Emily's recipe, appearing in the March 1995 issue of *Cobblestone*)

Ingredients

¼ cup butter of margarine

¼ cup heavy or whipping cream

½ cup molasses

2 cups flour

1 ½ teaspoons ground ginger

½ teaspoon baking soda

½ teaspoon salt

Granulated sugar or one egg, beaten

1. Preheat oven to 350 degrees. Grease a baking sheet.

2. Cream the butter or margarine, cream, and molasses in the bowl. Stir in the flour, ginger, baking soda, and salt.

3. Scoop up heaping tablespoonfuls of dough and shape them into flattened ovals about three inches long. (The dough will be sticky.) Place the ovals on the baking sheet.

4. To glaze the gingerbread, moisten the tops with water and sprinkle with granulated sugar, or brush the tops with beaten egg.

5. Bake for 20 minutes. Remove from the sheet and cool on the wire rack. Makes 12 large gingerbreads.

Put in a basket, ascend to upstairs bedroom, decorate with poetry, and lower by rope to children playing below.

II. Riddles

Emily Dickinson loved riddles, which she often wrote in the form of poems. Some of her riddles were about serious topics such as the passage of time and death; others were far more playful and childlike. Can you guess what this one is about?

I like to see it lap the miles,
And lick the valleys up,
And stop to feed itself at tanks;
And then, prodigious, step
Around a pile of mountains,
And, supercilious, peer
In shanties by the sides of roads;
And then a quarry pare
To fit its sides, and crawl between,
Complaining all the while
In horrid, hooting stanza;
Then chase itself down hill
And neigh like Boanerges;
Then, punctual as a star,
Stop—docile and omnipotent—
At its own stable door.

Write a short riddle just as Emily would have written it, by taking a bit of rhythm and adding a touch of rhyme. Your poem can be about anything from banana peels and iPods to global warming and animal rights. The sky is the limit. The sky, you say? "It blankets the earth, soft and blue" … You get the idea.

III. Amherst College

Amherst College, which was founded by Emily's grandfather, is today considered one of the leading liberal arts colleges in the nation. Who says? Well, there are literally hundreds of books and hundreds of Web sites that rank American colleges by such topics as the likeability of the professors, the size of the classes, the diversity of the student body, the win-loss record of the football and basketball teams, the pulse of the social life, the cleanliness of the dorm rooms, and the quality of the cafeteria food. Among the leading names are the *Princeton Review* and *Barron's Profiles of American Colleges*, whose reviews can be found online, in a bookstore, or at the library.

Take a look at some of the reviews about Amherst College. What are its strengths? How about its weaknesses? Does it sound like it would be a good fit for you? If you were to apply to just one college, which one would it be? Why? Your answer must include at least five thoughtfully explained reasons based on information gleaned from college reviews.

References

Books and Magazines

Denotes books and magazines of special interest to middle readers.

†*Denotes sources for quotations in this chapter.*

* Barth, Edna. *I'm Nobody! Who Are You? The Story of Emily Dickinson.* New York: Seabury Press, 1971.

* † Bolin, Frances Schoonmaker. *Poetry for Young People: Emily Dickinson.* New York: Sterling Publishing Co., 1994.

* † Chorlian, Med, ed. *Cobblestone's Emily Dickinson American Poet.* Petersborough, NH: Cobblestone, March 1995 issue.

* † Dommermuth-Costa, Carol. *Emily Dickinson: Singular Poet.* Minneapolis, MN: Lerner Publications Company, 1998.

Franklin, R. W., ed. *The Poems of Emily Dickinson.* Cambridge, MA: The Belknap Press of Harvard University Press, 1999.

* Hampson, Alfred Leete, ed. *Emily Dickinson: Poems for Youth.* Boston: Little, Brown and Company, 1996.

* Johnson, Thomas H. *The Complete Poems of Emily Dickinson.* Boston: Little, Brown and Company, 1960.

* Luce, William. *The Belle of Amherst: A Play Based on the Life of Emily Dickinson.* Boston: Houghton Mifflin Company, 1976.

* Spires, Elizabeth. *The Mouse of Amherst.* New York: Farrar, Straus & Giroux, 1999.

Additional Resources

Web Sites

Poems of Emily Dickinson: www.bartleby.com. Nearly 600 of Emily's poems are indexed by first lines.

Emily Dickinson Museum: www.emilydickinsonmuseum.org. Learn about the *Homestead* and the *Evergreens,* the two homes most closely associated with Emily and her family.

The Academy of American Poets: www.poets.org. At this website of the Academy of American Poets, visitors find thousands of poems as well as hundreds of poet biographies, essays, photographs, interviews, and poetry recordings.

Places to Visit in Amherst, Massachusetts

Emily Dickinson Museum. Take guided tours of the *Homestead* and the *Evergreens.*

Emily Dickinson Collection at the Jones Library of Amherst. Houses many of Emily's original poems and letters, family correspondence, newspaper clippings, photographs, and artwork.

Amherst College Archives and Special Collection. Includes many of Emily's original manuscripts, personal items, and letters to her best friend and sister-in-law, Susan Huntington Dickinson.

Videos

The Belle of Amherst. Kino Video, 1976.

Emily Dickinson: A Certain Slant of Light. Monterey Video, 1978.

Great Women Writers: Emily Dickinson. Kultur Video, 2001.

Illustration Credits

In the order photos appear in this chapter: 1. Wikimedia Commons. 2. Dr. William J. Ball, Department of Political Science, The College of New Jersey. 3. Wikipedia. 4. Courtesy of the Perry-Castaneda Library, University of Texas at Austin. 5. Wikipedia. 6. Perry-Castaneda Library, University of Texas at Austin.

Andrew Carnegie

1835–1919

Andrew Carnegie

Andrew Carnegie's life is one of the most inspiring "rags to riches" success stories of all time. As a young, poor, and uneducated Scottish immigrant living in Pittsburgh, he dreamed of being wealthy enough one day to own many books. His dream came true beyond his wildest expectations. Not only did he grow up to live in a castle housing his own library, he also built thousands of libraries for readers all over the world with his own money. "I believe that [a library] outranks any other thing that a community can do to benefit its people," he declared. "It is the never failing spring in the desert."

Most of Andrew's libraries were built in the United States, called by many of the day the "Land of Opportunity." He believed that a library offered immigrants and others on the low rung of the ladder the greatest opportunity of all to improve themselves. It just took work—hard work. "The fundamental advantage of a library is that it gives nothing for nothing," he once said. "Youths must acquire knowledge themselves. There is no escape from this."

Andrew "talked the talk and walked the walk." Because his family had so little money, he borrowed dozens of books from his friends in Pittsburgh and ever more from a local businessman. Books were his constant companion during his long climb up from a low-paid cotton-mill worker to multimillionaire steel tycoon, providing him with the education he was unable to obtain through formal schooling.

By the time Andrew sold the Carnegie Steel Corporation, he was the wealthiest man in the world. But what makes his story so inspiring is not so much the way he earned his fortune. Rather, it's what he did with his money after accumulating it. He gave almost all of it away to help others help themselves—through universities, museums, art galleries, theatres, hospitals, music halls and, of course, libraries. His legacy lives on to this day. In fact, the next time you visit a concert hall or view an art exhibit, don't be surprised if you hear or see the words: "Funded in part by the Carnegie Corporation."

To learn more about Andrew Carnegie's inspiring journey from rags to riches and from Captain of Industry to Patron Saint of Libraries, read his memoirs titled The Autobiography of Andrew Carnegie.

From *Readers and Leaders* by Susan Steffensen Romaine. Westport, CT: Libraries Unlimited.
Copyright © 2007 Libraries Unlimited.

Andrew Carnegie's birthplace in Dunfermline, Scotland

"To begin, then, I was born in Dunfermline [Scotland]," Andrew Carnegie wrote in his autobiography, "in the attic of a small one-story house, corner of Moodie Street and Priory Lane, on the 25th of November, 1835, and, as the saying is, *of poor but honest parents, of good kith and kin*." His father was a weaver; his mother managed a small grocery store and mended shoes. The Carnegies were not well-off, but they held steady to one very important belief—hard work pays off. "The richest heritage a young man can have is to be born into poverty," Andrew later said.

Andrew always had great respect for his parents, describing them as avid "readers and thinkers." When not weaving at his loom his father, William, could often be found poring over a book. In fact, William considered reading so important that he donated some of his own books to start a small borrowing library in Dunfermline. "It gave me great satisfaction to discover, many years later," Andrew wrote, "that my father was one of the five weavers in Dunfermline who gathered together the few books they had and formed the first circulating library in that town."

The library afforded the weavers endless hours of entertainment. To make the long shifts in the workshop pass more quickly, one weaver often read aloud from a book while the others worked. Andrew joined the reading circle as often as he could, especially when the books were about the history and heroes of Scotland.

Not until Andrew turned eight did he start school. "My parents had promised that I should never be sent to school until I asked leave to go," he wrote. When months then years passed and Andrew still showed no interest in enrolling, his parents finally turned to the schoolmaster, Robert Martin, for help. He shrewdly invited Andrew to his school on the best of all possible days—the day of a field trip. Andrew later remembered his parents' "great relief … when one day soon afterward I came and asked permission to go to Mr. Martin's school."

School was a "perfect delight" for Andrew. He breezed through reading, writing, and mathematics, earning the nickname "Martin's pet." He also developed a reputation for having a memory like an elephant. (As the saying goes, an elephant remembers *everything*.) Each morning during his "five or six minutes' slow walk" to school, Andrew memorized double verses from the Book of Psalms. After school, he committed to memory long passages from the poems of Scotland's Robert Burns and the works of English playwright William Shakespeare.

Robert Burns

Andrew's ability to "memorize anything whether it pleased me or not" paid off. The first penny he ever earned was for reciting before the school Robert Burns's lengthy poem, *Man Was Made to Mourn*. He later urged others to do the same. "I cannot name a more important means of benefiting young people than encouraging them to commit favorite pieces to memory and recite them often."

While well-schooled, Andrew learned his life lessons from his mother. Margaret Carnegie was "nurse, cook … teacher, saint, all in one," he said. She was also the rock that held the family together through some hard times.

Those hard times arrived when the Industrial Revolution swept across Great Britain, and machines and factories began replacing work done by hand at home. Like most other hand weavers, Andrew's father was suddenly thrown out of work by the steam-powered looms. "I began to learn what poverty meant," Andrew would later write. "It was burnt into my heart that my father had to beg for work."

Andrew's mother stepped in to help the family make ends meet. After finishing all her household chores during the day, she took in work from a local cobbler, stitching shoes late into the night. She also turned part of her husband's workshop into a small grocery store, selling flour, salt, cabbages, leeks, potatoes, tobacco, and candy. Throughout his life, Andrew was devoted to "that power that never failed in any emergency—my mother."

> Andrew was so devoted to his mother, he vowed he would never marry during her lifetime. He kept his promise, too. Just months after his mother died, fifty-one-year-old Andrew finally tied the knot to Louise Whitfield—whom he had secretly dated for seven years. A very patient woman, you might say. The wedding was small and simple, for Andrew believed that a fancy ceremony would be disrespectful of his mother's memory.

Still, the family struggled so hard to survive in Scotland, they finally had no choice but to sell all their possessions and set sail for America. Like so many other immigrants, the Carnegies hoped for a better life in this great Land of Opportunity, as depicted in these lyrics often sung by Andrew's father:

To the West, to the West, to the land of the free,
Where the Mighty Missouri rolls down to the sea;
Where a man is a man even though he must toil
And the poorest may gather the fruits of the soil.

The Carnegies settled in Allegheny City, Pennsylvania, across the river from Pittsburgh. Andrew's father quickly found work tending a large power-driven loom in a cotton mill. Thirteen-year-old Andrew joined him in the mill as a bobbin boy, replacing the large wooden spools on which the thread to make fabric was wound. "It was a hard life," Andrew admitted.

Child Laborers at Indiana Glass Works, 1908

Father and son would "rise and breakfast in the darkness, reach the factory before it was daylight, and, with a short interval for lunch, work till after dark." They toiled twelve hours a day, six days a week, in the hot, dusty, and noisy factory. For a week of hard labor, Andrew earned $1.20—or just a little more than a penny an hour. "The hours hung heavily upon me," he remembered, "and in the work itself I took no pleasure."

Fortunately, Andrew didn't labor in the dark cellar of the cotton mill for long. With a sharp mind and strong work ethic, he quickly advanced from bobbin boy to steam engine operator, and then to messenger boy in a telegraph office. He was overjoyed with his change in circumstances. In his own words, "My entrance into the telegraph office was a transition from darkness to light—from firing a small engine in a dark and dirty cellar into a clean office with bright windows and a literary atmosphere, with books, newspapers, pens, and pencils all around me. I was the happiest boy alive."

As a messenger boy in the telegraph office, Andrew quickly learned the lay of the land in Pittsburgh. He was rewarded for his prompt deliveries, sometimes with a pocketful of apples, oftentimes with a sweet cake. But the best reward of all was an occasional free ticket to the Pittsburgh Theatre. There, Andrew became acquainted "with the world that lay behind the green curtain," especially the world of William Shakespeare and "the magic that lay in his words." It was a turning point in Andrew's life. The playwright's "rhythm and melody all seemed to find a resting place in me," Andrew later explained.

From *Readers and Leaders* by Susan Steffensen Romaine. Westport, CT: Libraries Unlimited.
Copyright © 2007 Libraries Unlimited.

Andrew's busy schedule delivering telegraphs left little time for school, "nor did the wants of the family leave any money to spend on books." Yet in his spare time Andrew loved to read, both for pleasure and with an eye to self-improvement. Luckily, he learned of a Colonel James Anderson, a successful businessman in Allegheny City who opened the library in his home each Saturday afternoon to working boys in the neighborhood, allowing them to borrow a book from week to week.

Andrew Carnegie at age sixteen

There was just one glitch. Messenger boys were not considered "working boys with a trade," so the Colonel's library with some four hundred books was off limits to Andrew. Disappointed, Andrew asked the Colonel to kindly make an exception in a letter printed in the local newspaper and signed: *A working boy*.

The following week Colonel Anderson published his response in the *Pittsburgh Dispatch*, stating that he would make no exceptions. A rule was a rule.

Not to be deterred, Andrew pleaded his case in another letter to the newspaper, signing this one: *A working boy, though without a trade*. The colonel finally conceded with this simple request: *Will a working boy without a trade please call at my office.*

Andrew immediately phoned Colonel Anderson's office, and his life was forever changed. "The windows were opened in the walls of my dungeon through which the light of knowledge streamed in," he acknowledged.

Andrew soon became the library's most faithful patron. He regularly carried a book with him to work, which he read "during the intervals that could be snatched from duty." Among his favorites were Bancroft's *History of the United States*, essays by Macaulay and Lamb and, of course, the plays of William Shakespeare—all books that would have been very difficult for him to obtain elsewhere. "Only he who has longed as I did for Saturdays to come can understand what Colonel Anderson did for me and the boys of Allegheny. Is it any wonder that I resolved if ever surplus wealth came to me, I would use it imitating my benefactor?"

That surplus wealth did come Andrew's way, after founding the Carnegie Steel Company in Pittsburgh. It was the perfect time for steel—the years between the Civil War and World War I when the United States was becoming an industrial and world power. It was the perfect place, too, for Pittsburgh stood on a point of land where the Allegheny and Monongahela Rivers met to form the mighty Ohio River. Large ships transporting heavy steel beams dotted the Ohio River and nearby waterways.

Change could soon be seen almost everywhere. Rails made of Carnegie steel crisscrossed the nation, connecting one city to another. From New York to San Francisco, bridges and tall skyscrapers were built using girders and beams made of Carnegie steel. In shipyards, thick plates of Carnegie steel were welded together to make navy ships. On assembly lines in factories, Carnegie steel was used in motors and machines and turned into pipes, rods, tubes, wires, and pins. "Steel is king!" Andrew exclaimed.

> Did you eat breakfast and go to school today? If so, you probably used at least a dozen items made of steel. Kitchen appliances and cooking utensils are made of steel. Motors in cars and buses are, too. Scissors and staples have steel in them. As a matter of fact, steel beams form the very skeleton of many school buildings.

As the king of steel, Andrew was known to be ruthless in holding down costs and exhorted his employees to work long hours at low wages. His motto was, "Watch costs and the profits take care of themselves." And the profits did. The Carnegie Steel Company was soon producing more metal than all of the United Kingdom, with profits topping $40 million a year. Andrew rolled his profits right back into his business. "Put all your eggs in one basket and watch the basket," Andrew joked. "That's the way to make money."

Andrew Carnegie as a wealthy businessman

Over time, however, Andrew began to feel more and more uneasy about a life devoted to piling up cash. "To continue much longer overwhelmed by business cares and with most of my thoughts wholly upon the way to make more money in the shortest time, must degrade me beyond hope of permanent recovery. … I wish to spend the afternoons in receiving instruction and in reading systematically."

He did just that. With the help of private tutors, he studied literature, history, philosophy, economics, and French. He also sneaked away from his job for weeks and months at a time to read, write, and travel. "The rise and fall of iron and steel affecteth me not," he claimed. He first toured much of Europe and then journeyed literally all the way around the world.

Books were Andrew's steady companion during his travels. In China, he read the works of the great philosopher Confucius; in India, the teachings of Buddha. During the long days at sea, he pored over William Shakespeare's complete set of plays. Through his readings and travels, he came to believe that every people and culture has something of value to teach us. "No man has all that is best," he claimed, "neither is any [without] some advantages."

Along with reading, Andrew began writing about the great issues of his day. His most widely read book was called *Gospel of Wealth*, in which he laid out the responsibilities that come with owning a lot of money. Once a family has met its basic needs, he argued, all of its remaining wealth should be placed in a trust fund for the benefit of the community. In other words, Andrew believed that the well-to-do have a moral duty to take care of those who are less fortunate. In the most famous line from his book, the phrase for which he is now best remembered, Andrew wrote: "The man who dies rich, dies disgraced."

From *Readers and Leaders* by Susan Steffensen Romaine. Westport, CT: Libraries Unlimited.
Copyright © 2007 Libraries Unlimited.

J.P. Morgan

Andrew practiced what he preached in *Gospel of Wealth*. Just as impressively as he built his business and accumulated a vast fortune, he gave it all up. At age sixty-five, Andrew sold his Carnegie Steel Corporation to the banker J.P. Morgan for the astronomical sum of $480 million dollars, becoming overnight the richest man in the world. Andrew then turned all his energies to philanthropy—the giving away of his fortune to worthy causes. "I am not going to grow old piling up," Andrew insisted, "but in distributing."

Distribute he did. To promote the arts, he built Carnegie Hall in New York City, today one of the nation's most famous music halls. In education, he founded the Carnegie Institution in Washington, D.C.; the Carnegie Foundation for the Advancement of Teaching in Stanford, California; and the Carnegie Institute of Technology (now Carnegie-Mellon University) in Pittsburgh. He also established the Carnegie Endowment for International Peace to explore ways to resolve conflicts and prevent future wars. In addition, he created the Carnegie Hero Fund to reward those who risked their lives for others; a generous pension fund for hardworking teachers and college professors; and an organ fund to fill the rafters with music in thousands of churches all across the nation. "No man can become rich without first enriching others," he explained.

Perhaps more than any other cause, Andrew is best known for building thousands of public libraries all over the world, a gift that shaped the minds and lives of millions of people whom he never even met. He wrote: "It was from my own early experience that I decided there was no use to which money could be applied so productive … as the founding of a public library in a community."

Andrew donated his very first library to the place of his birth—Dunfermline, Scotland. His motto, "Let there be light," was carved in the entranceway. The beautiful stone castle with high ceilings and ornate windows announced to the world that the weaver's son had done well. "That my father was one of the founders of the first library in his native town, and that I have been fortunate enough to be founder of the last one, is certainly one of the most interesting incidents of my life," Andrew wrote in his autobiography.

Many more libraries followed. Andrew donated his second library to Braddock, Pennsylvania, to benefit the local steel mill's employees and their families, and his third to the people of his hometown, Allegheny City. Outside the library in Allegheny City, he poignantly built a monument in honor of Colonel James Anderson. Called *The Reading Blacksmith*, the monument commemorates Anderson's gift of opening his personal library to the working boys of the town.

From *Readers and Leaders* by Susan Steffensen Romaine. Westport, CT: Libraries Unlimited.
Copyright © 2007 Libraries Unlimited.

Soon after Allegheny, the City of Pittsburgh asked for and received a library. Today the Carnegie Library of Pittsburgh is part of a huge complex that includes a museum, an art gallery, technical schools, and a college.

All told, Andrew donated more than $56 million dollars to build 2,509 free public libraries in cities and towns throughout the English-speaking world. Nearly 2,000 of these Carnegie Libraries were constructed in the United States, with every state except Rhode Island having at least one of them. Many of these libraries are still around today. To ensure that the Carnegie Libraries "be free to the people forever," Andrew insisted that the words *Free Library* or *Free to the People* be carved in stone on the buildings.

Andrew explained his legacy this way: "If one [child] in each library district, by having access to one of these libraries, is half as much benefited as I was by having access to Colonel Anderson's four hundred well-worn volumes, I shall consider they have not been established in vain."

* * *

Just four months after walking his twenty-two-year-old daughter, Margaret, down the aisle at her wedding, Andrew Carnegie died at the age of eighty-three. By the time of his death, he had donated hundreds of millions of dollars to worthy causes. As this great philanthropist so simply and generously stated, "the sole purpose of being rich is to give away money."

With the remainder of his fortune, Andrew established a foundation called the Carnegie Corporation of New York. Today it is one of the top ten foundations in the country, carrying out Andrew's mission to "not make riches but usefulness your first aim." In this spirit of usefulness, may you always remember Andrew as he himself would want to be remembered—not so much as a Captain of Industry but as the Patron Saint of Libraries.

From *Readers and Leaders* by Susan Steffensen Romaine. Westport, CT: Libraries Unlimited.
Copyright © 2007 Libraries Unlimited.

Going the Extra Mile:
Extension Activities for Andrew Carnegie

I. Carnegie Hero Fund Commission

"I do not expect to stimulate or create heroism by this fund, knowing well that heroic action is impulsive; but I do believe that, if the hero is injured in his bold attempt to serve or save his fellows, he and those dependent upon him should not suffer pecuniarily."

—Andrew Carnegie

In 1904, in one of the worst mining disasters in U.S. history, a massive explosion in a coal mine near Pittsburgh claimed 181 lives. Two of the victims had courageously entered the mine after the explosion in ill-fated rescue attempts, sacrificing their lives in efforts to save others.

Deeply touched by this tragedy, Andrew Carnegie created the Carnegie Hero Fund Commission to recognize ordinary citizens who performed extraordinary acts of heroism. Over the years the commission has awarded some nine thousand bronze medals and nearly $30 million in grants to citizens who have risked their lives to save others. Daring rescue efforts have come in the face of floods, blizzards, assaults, fires, runaway vehicles, and even attacks by vicious animals. Fittingly, a verse from the New Testament of the Bible encircles the outer edge of each hero's bronze medal: "Greater love hath no man than this, that a man lay down his life for his friends" (John 15:13).

To learn more about these remarkable citizens, you can read the Carnegie Hero Fund Commission's recently published book titled, *A Century of Heroes* (edited by Douglas R. Chambers). Many more stories about winners of the prestigious Carnegie award can be found on the Internet. Pick just one hero and write a one-page description of his or her brave deed. Then share your stories with classmates to give well-deserved recognition to these modern-day heroes.

II. Androo Karnagy and Speling Wurdz

(Based on an Associated Press article dated July 5, 2006.)

Did you no that steel jiunt Androo Karnagy spent hundredz of thowzunz of dolarz trying to make speling simpler? That's right. He favored spelling based on phonetics, or sounds. He wanted to eliminate unpronounced vowels and double consonants. He also preferred the snappier writing in telegrams, which did not use conjunctions (and, but, as, because), prepositions (at, by, in, to, from, with), or articles (a, an, the).

Even though Andrew was a good speller, he saw the logic in simplified spelling. It would save printers time and money. It would save teachers and students countless headaches. But on an even bigger scale Andrew believed that simplified spelling would promote world peace, as nations could more readily resolve differences by communicating through just one language. In his essay titled "My Views about Improved Spelling," Andrew claimed that English would prevail as "the universal language, the most potent of all instruments for drawing the race together, ensuring peace and advancing civilization."

So about a century ago, Andrew created the Simplified Spelling Board, with the strong backing of Melvil Dewey (whom you will learn more about in Chapter 6). The board hoped to enlist fifty well-known writers who would agree to use simplified spelling in their writings—beginning with words such as *prolog, demogog, pedogog, tho, although, thoro, thorofare, thru*, and *thruout*. New words would be added to the list as the movement picked up steam.

Author Mark Twain jumped on the simplified spelling bandwagon, urging the Associated Press to "adopt and use our simplified forms and spread them to the ends of the earth." Playwright George Bernard Shaw, who mostly wrote in shorthand, set aside money in his will for the development of a new English alphabet. President Theodore Roosevelt tried to "make our spelling a little less foolish and fantastic" in all White House memos. The *Chicago Tribune* also got into the act, using simpler spelling in its newspaper for four decades.

Despite this backing, the idea of simplified spelling never really captivated the masses. "I think that the average person simply did not see this as a needed change or a necessary change or something that was … going to change their lives for the better," claimed a librarian at the Carnegie Library of Pittsburgh.

The one exception has been electronic mail and text messages. Andrew Carnegie died in 1919, well before the advent of the computer and the cell phone. Had he lived, he probably would have been thrilled knowing that millions of Americans send electronic messages each day using their own forms of simplified spelling. To give just one example, "Hav a gr8 day!"

Write your own instant message to a friend (about a paragraph in length) using as much simplified spelling as you can. Then see if a friend can decipher the message. If so, Andrew wuud hav bin very pleezd.

III. The Johnny Appleseed of Libraries in Asia

(Based on a *San Francisco Chronicle* article dated September 26, 2004, "Rich in Books: Like Andrew Carnegie before him, former Microsoft executive John Wood is building libraries—more than 1,000 since 1998—but in southern Asia.")

Carrying on Andrew Carnegie's legacy today is John Wood, who is building thousands of libraries throughout impoverished areas of Asia. Here is his inspiring story:

After raking in millions of dollars as a top executive with Microsoft, John Wood decided one day that he wanted more out of life. He quit his job, strapped on his hiking gear, and headed off to the mountains of Nepal. While hiking through the mountains, he met a headmaster who invited him to tour his school in a nearby village. John was shocked by what he saw: overcrowded classrooms, crumbling chalkboards, dim lighting, and a library with no children's books. When John asked the headmaster how he managed with no reading materials for 450 kids, the response was: "Perhaps, sir, you could help us get more books."

So began John Wood's calling to become the Johnny Appleseed of school libraries in Asian villages. "As it happened, I spent the rest of my evenings on the trek reading books on Buddhism, including the Dalai Lama's teachings about the value of bringing education to the disadvantaged," John recalled. "So working on literacy found me more than I found it." He planted the first seeds by sending an e-mail to one hundred friends, asking for donations of new and used children's books. To his surprise, he received 3,000 books in the first month alone.

Next came the delivery of the books to schools halfway around the world. Even for a technological guru, the logistics were overwhelming. For the first leg of the journey, John shipped thirty-seven boxes of books to Katmandu, Nepal. He then loaded the boxes on a bus heading toward a hiking trail in the Himalayas. At the trail, John strapped the heavy boxes on the backs of six donkeys and, many miles and days later, hand-delivered the books to ten village schools.

The deliveries were so rewarding that John returned to the United States and launched Room to Read, a nonprofit company in the business of putting smiles on the faces of book-loving kids throughout Asia. Room to Read has now opened over one thousand libraries in Nepal, Vietnam, Cambodia, and India.

"Andrew Carnegie built 1,700 free libraries, but nobody has done anything like that in the Third World," says Wood. "That's why our work is so exciting. It's an investment in literacy, like Carnegie's, that will pay dividends for generations to come."

Like Andrew Carnegie, John Wood thinks big. He would like to double the number of libraries in Asia each year, helping ten million kids learn to read by 2010. You can help him out by gathering up used books around your house and mailing them to Room to Read, The Presidio, P.O. Box 29127, San Francisco, CA 94129.

If you would like to learn more about John Wood, read his memoirs titled *Leaving Microsoft to Change the World: An Entrepreneur's Odyssey to Educate the World's Children.*

References

Books, Magazines, and Newspapers

Denotes books and magazines of special interest to middle readers.
†Denotes sources for quotations in this chapter.

* Bowman, John S. *Andrew Carnegie: Steel Tycoon*. Englewood Cliffs, NJ: Silver Burdett Press, 1989.

* † Carnegie, Andrew. *The Autobiography of Andrew Carnegie*. Boston: Northeastern University Press, 1986 (reprinting).

* † Cooper, Bob. "*Rich in Books:* Like Andrew Carnegie before Him, Former Microsoft Executive John Wood Is Building Libraries—More Than 1,000 Since 1998—but in Southern Asia," *San Francisco Chronicle*, September 26, 2004.

* † Hakim, Joy. *An Age of Extremes* (Book 8 in A History of US series). New York: Oxford University Press, 2005.

* Jones, Theodore. *Carnegie Libraries Across America*. New York: John Wiley & Sons, 1997.

* † Kent, Zachary. *Andrew Carnegie: Steel King and Friend to Libraries*. Springfield, NJ: Enslow Publishers, 1999.

* Meltzer, Milton. *The Many Lives of Andrew Carnegie*. New York: Franklin Watts, 1997.

Nasaw, David. *Andrew Carnegie*. New York: Penguin Press, 2006.

Wall, Joseph Frazier. *Andrew Carnegie*. New York: Oxford University Press, 1970.

* † Walsh, Glenn A., ed. *Cobblestone's Andrew Carnegie: From Poor Immigrant to Wealthy Philanthropist*. Peterborough, NH: Cobblestone, April 1999 issue.

Additional Resources

Web Sites

The Carnegie Corporation of New York: www.carnegie.com. As one of the nation's largest foundations, the Carnegie Foundation carries on Andrew's legacy of giving away millions and millions of dollars to worthy causes.

Carnegie Libraries: The Future Made Bright: www.cr.nps.gov/NR/TWHP/wwwlps/lessons/ 50carnegie/50carnegie.htm. A classroom-ready lesson plan showing students the way in which Andrew blended aggressive business practices with generous gift-giving, focusing on his role in building thousands of public libraries all across the nation.

Andrew Carnegie: A Tribute: www.clpgh.org/exhibit/carnegie.html. This site uses many of Andrew's own quotes and writings to give a better picture of the man and his legacy.

Places to Visit in Pittsburgh, Pennsylvania

The Carnegie Museum of Art. Houses important collections of nineteenth- and twentieth-century American and European paintings, sculptures, and photographs.

The Carnegie Museum of Natural History. Holds major collections on geology, botany, and archaeology as well as a 150,000-volume library of reference materials.

The Carnegie Science Center. A hands-on setting with a planetarium, theatres, a computer learning lab, a submarine, and various collections on science and technology.

Videos

Empires of Industry: Andrew Carnegie and the Age of Steel. A&E Home Video, 1997.

America's Castles—Andrew Carnegie: Skibo. A&E Home Video, 2006.

Illustration Credits

In the order photos appear in this chapter: 1. Perry-Castaneda Library, University of Texas at Austin. 2. Wikimedia Commons. 3. Perry-Castaneda Library, University of Texas at Austin. 4. Dr. William J. Ball, Department of Political Science, The College of New Jersey. 5. Wikimedia Commons. 6. Wikimedia Commons. 7. Perry-Castaneda Library, University of Texas at Austin.

Thomas Alva Edison

1847–1931

Thomas Alva Edison

Just a handful of clever minds have made gigantic contributions toward books and libraries. Johannes Gutenberg invented the printing press, which for the first time allowed books to be reproduced in huge quantities. Benjamin Franklin founded the nation's first library, and Andrew Carnegie donated some $50 million toward the building of free public libraries, so that books could be freely exchanged among friends and neighbors. Melvil Dewey helped to organize libraries with the Dewey Decimal System, making it much easier to hunt down books on library shelves. Louis Braille developed a new form of writing with raised dots, so that people who are blind could read.

Then there's Thomas Edison. Wait a minute … Thomas Edison? What does he have to do with reading? The answer: plenty. Tom invented the electric lightbulb, allowing people to read at night without requiring light from a fireplace or candle. Too, no longer were they forced to light up their rooms with dangerous and smelly gas lamps. Instead, all it took was the simple flick of a switch. With the electric lightbulb, kids could curl up in bed at night and flip through pages and pages of cliff-hanging adventures or nail-biting mysteries until they heard those all too familiar words: "LIGHTS OUT!"

The electric lightbulb has profoundly changed our lives, as have some of Tom's other inventions—the phonograph, ancestor of today's CD and DVD players; the movie camera, which gave rise to today's huge movie industry; and the first central power plant to generate the electricity needed for Tom's lightbulbs. What's more, his way of working with teams of scientists became the model for the modern research laboratory. No wonder Thomas Edison is sometimes dubbed the "Wizard of Menlo Park," the world's first research park where he carried out many of his experiments.

But don't think all this success came easily to the Wizard. To the contrary, he suffered countless setbacks and disappointments while conducting thousands upon thousands of experiments in his laboratory. He persevered by looking upon "failed" experiments as opportunities to glean new information and set his research on entirely different paths. "Negative results are just what I want," he claimed. "They're just as valuable to me as positive results. I can never find the thing that does the job best until I find the ones that don't do."

For more inspiring quotes by the Wizard, read the National Geographic's Inventing the Future: A Photobiography of Thomas Alva Edison *by Marfe Ferguson Delano.*

It is obvious that we don't know one millionth of one percent about anything.

—Thomas Edison

Thomas Alva Edison was born on a cold winter day in the snow-swept port of Milan, Ohio. Nicknamed Little Al, he was a frail baby with an unusually large head. His head was so big that his doctor feared brain fever, an infection that could lead to death. Fortunately, Little Al survived—as he would in the face of many other obstacles in life.

Al was a bright and curious child, some calling him a nervous little question box. He was constantly asking grown-ups how different things worked. Why could you see a hammer hit a board from a distance before you could hear it? How did steam make a train move? How did telegraph wires carry messages? If the adults didn't know the answer, he'd look them straight in the eye and ask, "Why *don't* you know?"

Sometimes Al's curiosity got the best of him. He watched hens sit on eggs until they hatched and thought to himself, "Hey, I can do that, too." The result was a wet and slimy seat on his pants. Checking out a bumblebee's nest one day, he was suddenly attacked by an angry ram. While experimenting with new ways to shorten a strap on his skate, he accidentally cut off the tip of his finger with an axe.

Then there was the time Al became convinced birds could fly because they ate worms. He just couldn't get the cockamamie idea out of his head. So he mixed mashed worms with water and gave the drink to a friend to prove she would take flight. Not! She got sick to her stomach, and Al got spanked on his bottom. He was punished again when he set fire to his father's barn to "just see what it would do." At least he had the good sense to start the fire when all the animals were out to pasture.

Surprises and reverses can serve as an incentive for great accomplishment.

—Thomas Edison

Al moved to Port Huron, Michigan, where he attended a noisy, one-room public school with forty students ranging in age from five to twenty-one. Because of the many different ages, there were lots of rules about punctuality, obedience, and discipline—all areas where curious, chatty, and careless Al came up short. Let's just say, school wasn't exactly his strong point.

For one thing, Al's habit of asking lots of questions in class annoyed his teacher, Mr. Crawford. In addition, Al tended to draw and doodle in his notebook while other students memorized their lessons. "I remember I [was] never … able to get along at school," Al would later say. "I was always at the foot of the class. I used to feel that teachers did not sympathize with me."

Al was often disciplined by Mr. Crawford, who donned a long, black frock coat and carried a big pointer that he used to hit unruly students. But not even the threat of being bopped over the head with the pointer could bring Al in step with his classmates. After twelve weeks of school, Mr. Crawford finally gave up on him. "One day," Al recalled, "I heard the teacher tell the visiting school inspector that I was *addled* [easily confused] and it would not be worthwhile keeping me in school any longer. I was so hurt by this last straw that I burst out crying and went home and told my mother about it."

Nancy Edison reassured her son that his brains were in no way "addled." Quite the opposite, Al was *so* bright and creative that he was easily bored by memorizing facts and practicing penmanship at school. He needed more challenge not less, Nancy reasoned, showing a confidence in her son that he never forgot: "She was the most enthusiastic champion a boy ever had, and I determined right then that I would be worthy of her, and show her that her confidence had not been misplaced. … I was always a careless boy, and with a mother of different mental caliber I should have probably turned out badly. But her firmness, her sweetness, her goodness, were potent powers to keep me in the right path."

Inventors must be poets so that they may have imagination.

—Thomas Edison

It is very likely that Al's troubles in school stemmed from a learning disability now known as *dyslexia*. Have you heard of that before? It comes from *dys,* which means bad or difficult, and *lexia,* which means word. Hav ingbys lexiac anwake it harbtoreab. Translation: Having dyslexia can make it hard to read.

> In just about every classroom in America, one or two children have dyslexia. While many of these children struggle in school, they often find their creative niche and go on to pursue very successful careers in science, sports, politics, arts, and entertainment. Famous dyslexics include Muhammad Ali, Hans Christian Andersen, Alexander Graham Bell, Cher, Winston Churchill, Tom Cruise, Leonardo da Vinci, Walt Disney, Albert Einstein, Henry Ford, Whoopi Goldberg, Magic Johnson, John Kennedy, John Lennon, Pablo Picasso, and Woodrow Wilson.

People with dyslexia can see just fine. The problem is the way the brain interprets what the eyes see. Because the brain has difficulty absorbing details received from the eye's optic nerves, letters may appear backward, upside down, jumbled up, bunched together, or even jumping around on a page. Writing that looks just fine to you—if you don't have dyslexia—might look like this to someone with dyslexia:

The word sare n otsp aced cor rect ly.

We spel wrds xatle az tha snd to us.

Sometimesthelettersarepushedtogether.

The good news is that for the very same reason that kids with dyslexia overlook details, they often excel at problem solving and have an amazing ability to grasp the big picture—that is to say, to see the forest through the trees. As an example, take a look at these two words:

TORNADO
VOLCANO

When reading, a dyslexic may confuse one word for the other because of the three shared letters—the *o, a,* and the *o.* Yet when asked what a volcano does, a child with dyslexia will correctly answer, "It erupts and spews hot lava."

While Nancy Edison didn't have a name for it at the time, she fortunately saw right through Al's learning disability and recognized his untapped brilliance. That begged the question, How was this doting mother going to unleash her son's genius? As a first step, homeschooling. Trained as a teacher, Nancy insisted that "no fetters hobble the free rein, the full sweep of his imagination." She began with the Bible and the 3 Rs (reading, 'riting, and 'rithmetic), and then charted a course through literature, history, science, and geography.

It was a fun voyage made happier by the stacks of books that Al devoured along the way. "My mother taught me how to read good books quickly and correctly, and as this opened up a great world in literature, I have always been very thankful for the early training," he remembered.

From *Readers and Leaders* by Susan Steffensen Romaine. Westport, CT: Libraries Unlimited.
Copyright © 2007 Libraries Unlimited.

Charles Dickens

Among the treasures mother and son discovered together were history books such as *History of England, Decline and Fall of the Roman Empire,* and *History of the World,* as well as great works in literature by Charles Dickens and William Shakespeare. Al especially liked Shakespeare and became so excited by his plays that he considered becoming an actor when he grew up. But because of his high-pitched voice and painful shyness, he quickly gave up the idea. We can now say that the world is a better and brighter place because of it.

Sometimes, all you need to invent something is a good imagination and a pile of junk.

—Thomas Edison

Al's eyes really lit up when he got his hands on his first science book. Called *A School Compendium of Natural and Experimental Philosophy,* Al later said it was "the first book of science I read when a boy, nine years old, the first I could understand."

The book was full of experiments, which Al soaked up like a sponge. But just reading about the experiments was not enough. Al wanted to conduct them—every single one of those experiments—so that he could see for himself exactly how things worked.

To get started, Al built a makeshift laboratory in the basement of his house. He stocked his lab with all kinds of neat stuff he had found at the town dump—mercury, feathers, sulfur, beeswax, alum, and cornstalk pitch. He added to his collection some cheap chemicals he bought from the town pharmacist. Soon he had more than two hundred bottles of all sizes, shapes, and colors, many of which he carefully labeled with the letters *P-O-I-S-O-N* so no one would dare touch them.

For hours, Al locked himself in the dark room beneath his house, puttering with wires, test tubes filled with colorful powders, a Bunsen burner, rubber hoses, acids, and gases. As he tinkered away, he read aloud to himself from thick volumes of science and math books such as Fresenius' *Qualitative Analysis.* Nasty smells sometimes seeped out of his basement. Thuds and explosions occasionally shook the house. But through it all, Al concentrated on his experiments, breaking away just long enough to indulge in his favorite snack—a slice of his mother's homemade apple pie and a glass of milk. Then he was right back to work again.

Al kept up this same routine as an adult. He had a habit of working nights, so around midnight he would break for a meal, often just a piece of cake or pie and a glass of milk, before resuming his laboratory experiments.

The happiest time in my life was when I was twelve years old. I was just old enough to have a good time in the world, but not old enough to understand any of its troubles.

—Thomas Edison

By age twelve, Al was eager to explore the "wide worlds out there beyond Port Huron." And so it was that Al's homeschooling came to an end and he got his first job as a newsboy, selling newspapers and candy to passengers aboard the Grand Trunk Railway.

Al put in a very busy day with the Grand Trunk. The train departed Port Huron each morning at 7 o'clock, arrived three hours later in Detroit, and after a long stopover returned to Port Huron that evening at 9 o'clock. Count up the hours in Al's work day. It's a lot!

Many years later Al said, "Personally, I enjoy working about 18 hours a day. Besides the short catnaps I take each day, I average about four to five hours of sleep per night."

During the train ride, Al walked up and down the aisles selling all kinds of goodies. For fellow readers, he offered newspapers, magazines, guidebooks, joke books, and dime novels (which he always read before selling). For those passengers interested in a light snack, Al's menu included chewing gum, candy, peanuts, popcorn, fruit, and sandwiches. Sales were usually brisk.

Al showed his true character during the Grand Trunk's long layovers in Detroit. Now, be honest. What would *you* do if you had a few hours of spare time each afternoon? Play ball? Go to a skate park? Relax with Nintendo? Hang out with friends at a nearby McDonald's? Watch a movie? Shop at a mall? Al, who was once described as having "had no boyhood days," was way too restless simply to hang out with friends during the eight-hour layovers. Instead, he spent his spare time browsing through books at the library.

Sir Isaac Newton

"My refuge was the Detroit Public Library," Al explained years later. "I started, it now seems to me, with the first book on the bottom shelf and went through the lot, one by one. I didn't read a few books, I read the library." (This feat he later shared with Harry Truman.) Among the books Al devoured was Isaac Newton's *Principia Mathematica,* a "bible" for budding scientists. He also poured over *The World Dictionary of Science,* Thomas Burton's *Anatomy of Melancholy,* and all the chemistry books he could get his hands on.

Even though I am nearly deaf, I seem gifted with a kind of inner hearing which enables me to detect sounds and noises which the ordinary listener does not hear.

—Thomas Edison

All this reading at the Detroit Public Library gave Al some new ideas for science experiments. His job afforded him a small allowance for new lab supplies. Unfortunately, he was traveling so much, he rarely had time at home to conduct his experiments. So Al begged and pleaded and finally persuaded the Grand Trunk's conductor to let him build a small laboratory in the train's baggage car.

Everything went smoothly until one day, during a bumpy ride, a jar containing a dangerous substance called phosphorous fell from a shelf, burst into flames, and spread throughout the baggage car. The irate conductor, a Scotsman, yanked Al up by the ears and shouted, "Off ye go, lock, stock, and ivry drap o' chemicals with ye. Ah must 'been daft when Ah let ye br-r-ring thim aboord!"

Years later Al blamed the hot-tempered, ear-pulling conductor for causing his early hearing loss. More likely, it was chronic ear infections or a childhood case of scarlet fever. Whatever the cause, by the time Al turned twelve, he "could not hear a bird sing." He couldn't hear much of anything. "Broadway is as quiet to me as a country village is to a person with normal hearing," he admitted.

Al never sulked about his hearing loss. In some ways he even considered his near deafness a blessing, for it allowed him to tune out bothersome noises and idle chitchat so he could better concentrate on what he really wanted to do: read, think, experiment, and discover. And so it was that Al happily retreated into the quieter worlds of libraries and laboratories. In fact, he later turned down an operation that might have restored his hearing, for he was afraid he "would have difficulty re-learning how to channel [my] thinking in an ever more noisy world."

Samuel F. Morse

Opportunity is missed by most people because it is dressed in overalls and looks like work.

—Thomas Edison

At fifteen, the budding inventor made clear that he preferred to be called Tom. His name was not all that was new. He developed a newfound interest in the telegraph, a system of wires through which messages could be sent back and forth using small bursts of electricity. Using an illustration in a science book, Tom constructed his own telegraph by stretching a wire from his home to a friend's house about half a mile away. He and his friend later spent hours and hours tapping out messages to one another using the dots and dashes of the Morse Code. (See "Talk by Lightning" in the Extension Activities.)

> The Morse Code always had a special place in Thomas Edison's heart. He proposed to the woman of his dreams by tapping dots and dashes into the palm of her hand. Her response? "The word *yes* is an easy one to send in telegraphic signals, and she sent it," Tom happily reported. Believe it or not, he even nicknamed his first two children *Dot* and *Dash*.

Tom soon snagged a well-paying job at a local telegraph office. When he wasn't sending or receiving messages, he relaxed by reading back issues of *Scientific American*. Sometimes he became so occupied reading a magazine article that he would let messages pile up for hours before clearing his "in box."

Tom also sneaked out of the telegraph office on occasion to visit the nearest library, seeking out every book he could get his hands on regarding the telegraph. These included *History and Practice of the Electric Telegraph, Electric Telegraph, Handbook of Practical Telegraphy,* and *Electric Telegraph Manipulation.* "I can never pick up anything without wishing to improve it," Tom admitted. This was just the beginning of his lifelong love of tinkering and inventing, a passion that would soon bring him both fame and fortune.

I find out what the world needs. Then I go ahead and try to invent it.

—Thomas Edison

Tom's most productive years as an inventor were spent in Menlo Park, New Jersey, where he basically invented the business of inventing. That is, he brought together teams of scientists and engineers at what he called his "invention factory" but what later became known as the world's very first research laboratory. Together they patented 1,093 inventions, a feat that has never been matched by another inventor to this day. It was here that Tom was first referred to as the "Wizard of Menlo Park." With typical modesty he said, "If he was a wizard at anything, it was surrounding himself with the best."

> Besides "Wizard of Menlo Park," Tom could have been called "Mayor of Crazy Town." He rarely combed his hair, which turned white when he was only twenty-three years old. In addition, he often spat tobacco juice out of the side of his mouth; his clothes were usually dirty; he bathed just once a week; and he didn't believe in exercise. "Most of the exercise I get is from standing and walking all day from one laboratory table to another. I derive more benefit from this than some of my friends and competitors get from playing games like golf."

A list of the Wizard's most important inventions would be too long to fit on a single page. His favorite was the phonograph, a machine that could record and play back sound. (In case you're wondering, the very first words ever recorded were of Tom singing, *Mary had a little lamb, its fleece was white as snow ....*) He called this talking machine "my baby," saying it would "grow up to be a big feller and support me in my old age." How prophetic he was, as the phonograph has since evolved into today's CD and DVD players.

Thomas Edison with phonograph

Al's most difficult invention was the electric lightbulb. "I speak without exaggeration when I say that I have considered three thousand theories in connection with electric light," he maintained. He also made important contributions to the telegraph, telephone, stock ticker, car battery, microphone, movie camera, typewriter, waxed paper, electric pen, vote recorder, fire and burglar alarm, mimeograph machine—the list goes on and on. (To learn more, see "Inventing the Future" in the Extension Activities.)

Thomas Edison's first lightbulb

At one point a headline appeared in a New York newspaper boasting, "Edison Invents a Machine That Will Feed the Human Race—[Making] Biscuits, Meat, Vegetables, and Wine out of Air, Water, and Common Earth." Many read it and were astounded. Was "The Wizard" so brilliant that he had even found a solution to world hunger? Well, not exactly. The headline appeared on April 1, 1878 … April Fool's Day.

Genius is one percent inspiration and ninety-nine per cent perspiration. Accordingly, a genius is often merely a talented person who has done all of his or her homework.

—Thomas Edison

There are workhorses and there are workhorses. Just about everyone would agree that Tom was the crème de la crème of workhorses. To invent at such a furious pace, he often worked through the night, napping a few minutes here and there—either sitting in a chair or lying on top of or under tables with the crook of his elbow for a pillow. He eventually built a cabinet in his lab just large enough for one person, where he could hide away to take a catnap. "He invents all the time, even in his sleep," his wife once said.

As hard as he pushed himself, Tom was just as demanding of his workers. He called them "muckers" and he, himself, was the "Chief Mucker." Muck is usually thought of as mud or filth, which is exactly how Tom thought of inventing. Hard and messy.

If Tom were close to a discovery, he expected his "muckers" to stay long into the night, weekends as well as weekdays. Their only break was when Tom sat down at his pipe organ and everyone joined in for a sing-along. Once, when an exhausted worker fell asleep on the job, Tom jolted him awake with an electrical shock. "I never did anything worth doing by accident," Tom explained, "nor did any of my inventions come by accidents. … They were achieved by having trained myself to be analytical and to endure and tolerate hard work." He expected much the same of his "muckers," whom he sometimes dubbed the "Insomnia Squad" because they put in so many sleepless nights.

When not inventing, Tom relaxed, as he had throughout his life, by reading. He kept an account at Brentano's bookstore and was known to order hundreds of dollars worth of books each month, a huge sum in those days. If he came across a topic that interested him, he'd call Brentano's and ask for every single book and magazine on the subject, for immediate delivery.

Along with his insatiable appetite for books, Tom maintained a highly unusual appetite for food in the last few years of his life. Adhering strictly to a fad diet, he "consumed nothing more than a pint of milk every three hours," certain that this milk-only diet would eventually restore his health.

Thomas Edison's eighty-second birthday party, left to right: President Herbert Hoover, Henry Ford, Edison, and Harvey Firestone

If we did all the things we are really capable of doing, we would literally astound ourselves.

—Thomas Edison

Thomas Alva Edison was once asked when he would retire. "The day before the funeral," he replied. His prediction turned out to be a good one. At his laboratory, he punched in and punched out with his own time card every day until just before he died at age eighty-four.

Upon hearing the news, America mourned. On the evening of his funeral, at precisely 10:00 P.M. Eastern time, the nation plunged into darkness as Americans celebrated Tom's life by turning off their lights for one full minute. Even the Statute of Liberty's torch was darkened. In doing so, the country honored a man who had profoundly changed the world through a lifetime of bright ideas and inventions.

Going the Extra Mile:
Extension Activities for Thomas Edison

I. "Talk by Lightning"

Dot-dot-dot-dot. Dot. Dot-dash-dot-dot. Dot-dash-dot-dot. Dash-dash-dash. That's Morse Code for hello. Named after the American inventor Samuel Morse, Morse Code is the "software" behind the telegraph—allowing people to communicate messages quickly and across great distances long before the telephone, fax, and email came into existence. Messages sent in Morse Code sound like a series of clicks, as the flow of electricity through a wire is started and stopped over and over again. A click followed by a short interval is called a dot. A click followed by a long interval is a dash. As shown below, each letter of the alphabet has its own dot-and-dash combination.

Alphabet in Morse Code

A	. -	N	- .
B	- . . .	O	- - -
C	- . - .	P	. - - .
D	- . .	Q	- - . -
E	.	R	. - .
F	. . - .	S	. . .
G	- - .	T	-
H	. . . .	U	. . -
I	. .	V	. . . -
J	. - - -	W	. - -
K	- . - .	X	- . . -
L	. - . .	Y	- . - -
M	- -	Z	- - . .

The Morse Code was originally used to check on weather conditions in different parts of the country, to see whether trains were running on schedule, and to send distress signals from sea (originally coded as "CQD" but later as "SOS"). It was later nicknamed "talk by lightning" and became a quick and inexpensive way to communicate all kinds of information across long distances. Using the Morse Code alphabet, see if you can decode this little tidbit:

You can make your own telegraph for sending a message in Morse Code to a friend. All it takes is a quick trip to a hardware store, a bit of help from a parent or older sibling, and lots of patience. To get started, visit www.yesmag.bc.ca/projects/telegraph.html. By the time you have connected all of the wires and buzzers, you'll be able to "talk by lightning" with friends just as Tom did some hundred years ago.

II. Inventing the Future

Tom Edison never stopped doing. To learn more about this prolific inventor and his creative mind, here's a game for you. Surf the Internet to match the names of Edison's inventions appearing in the left column with their descriptions found in the right column.

Message in Morse Code: A Good Friend Is Life's Brightest Light

Invention	Description
____ 1. Vote recorder	a. For this most challenging of all his inventions, Edison sketched hundreds of designs and tested more than 1,600 materials.
____ 2. Alkaline battery	b. After the invention of this "baby," Edison became an overnight celebrity and was proclaimed the "Inventor of the Age." He was less sure of his success, admitting, "I was always afraid of things that worked the first time."
____ 3. Stock ticker	c. Edison's first invention and his only real flop. He later concluded, "Anything that won't sell, I don't want to invent."
____ 4. Movie camera	d. After an advertisement claimed it could produce "5,000 copies from a single writing," lawyers and mapmakers snatched it up.
____ 5. Lightbulb	e. This invention came right on the heels of the phonograph. When a crank was turned, words to nursery rhymes were "spoken."
____ 6. Phonograph	f. Thanks to this invention, the speaker's voice over the telephone was louder and clearer, later leading to the development of the microphone.
____ 7. Carbon telephone transmitter	g. It became Edison's biggest moneymaker, lighting railway cars and ships and powering torpedoes during World War I.
____ 8. Electric pen	h. It was described as "an instrument which does for the eye what the phonograph does for the ear."
____ 9. Talking doll	i. Named after the loud noise it made, this invention sent minute-by-minute reports of the price of gold to stockbrokers.
____ 10. Power station	j. The Wizard himself rolled up his sleeves and dug trenches to lay cables for this invention.

Answers: 1c, 2g, 3i, 4h, 5a, 6b, 7f, 8d, 9e, 10j

III. WHATISITLIKETOHAVEDYSLEXIA?

What is dyslexia? What are some of the causes of this learning disability? How is it diagnosed? Does dyslexia run in families? How does it affect a child's ability to read? Are boys just as likely to have dyslexia as girls? What is being done to help kids with dyslexia? To get answers to these questions, interview at least one student at your school with dyslexia and at least one reading teacher who works with students with dyslexia. You may also want to check out two Web sites, http://kidshealth. org/teen/school-jobs/school/dyslexia.html and http://staff.washington.edu/chudler/dyslexia.html. Once you have gathered up all of your information, write an article for your school newspaper raising awareness about dyslexia and the special challenges it poses for some of the students at your school.

References

Books and Magazines

Denotes books and magazines of special interest to middle readers.

†*Denotes sources for quotations in this chapter.*

* Adair, Gene. *Thomas Alva Edison: Inventing the Electric Age.* New York: Oxford University Press, 1996.

* Adler, David A. *Thomas Alva Edison: Great Inventor.* New York: Holiday House, 1990.

* † Chorlian, Meg, ed. *Cobblestone's Thomas Alva Edison: American Wizard.* Peru, IL: Carus, December 2005 issue.

* Cramer, Carol. *Thomas Edison.* San Diego: Greenhaven Press, 2001.

* † Delano, Marfe Ferguson. *Inventing the Future: A Photobiography of Thomas Alva Edison.* Washington, DC: National Geographic Society, 2002.

* Dooling, Michael. *Young Thomas Edison.* New York: Holiday House, 2005.

* Morgan, Nina. *Thomas Edison.* New York: Bookwright Press, 1991.

* Murcia, Rebecca Thatcher. *Thomas Edison: Great Inventor (Uncharted, Unexplored, and Unexplained).* Hockessin, DE: Mitchell Lane, 2004.

* Parker, Steve. *Thomas Edison and Electricity.* New York: HarperCollins, 1992.

* † Sullivan, George. *In Their Own Words: Thomas Edison.* New York: Scholastic, 2001.

* Wallace, Joseph. *The Lightbulb.* New York: Atheneum Books for Young Readers, 1999.

Additional Resources

Web Sites

Thomas A. Edison Papers, Rutgers University: http://edison.rutgers.edu/. Housed here are more than five million pages of documents giving rare insight into Tom's creative genius.

Thomas Edison's Home Page: www.thomasedison.com/. This site is chock-full of the inventor's quotes. It also contains his biography, a photo gallery, and a timeline of major inventions and events in his life.

Edison National Historic Site: www.nps.gov/edis/home.htm. Find links to "Edisonia" and "Edifun," take a tour of the Edison's Glenmont home, and see his family's photo album.

The Library of Congress's American Memory: http://memory.loc.gov/ammem/edhtml/edhome. html. View the films Edison created included one in which he actually appeared.

Places to Visit

Edison Birthplace Museum in Milan, Ohio. The house where Tom was born and a museum featuring some of his many inventions.

Edison & Ford Winter Estates in Fort Myers, Florida. Thomas Edison and Henry Ford owned summer homes in Florida right next door to one another. Their houses and surrounding gardens as well as one of Edison's labs are on the grounds and open to the public.

Edison National Historic Site in West Orange, New Jersey. Along with his Glenmont home and West Orange laboratory, visitors can find many of Tom's important papers, photographs, and sound recordings.

Henry Ford Museum & Greenfield Village in Dearborn, Michigan. The restoration of Tom's Menlo Park laboratory housing many of the original artifacts.

Videos

Biography: Thomas A. Edison—Father of Invention. A&E Home Video, 2006.

Edison—The Invention of the Movies (1891–1918). Kino Video, 2005.

Edison's Miracle of Light. The American Experience. Public Broadcasting Service, 1995.

The Edison Effect. The History Channel. A&E Television Networks, 1995.

Illustration Credits

In the order photos appear in this chapter: 1. Perry-Castaneda Library, University of Texas at Austin. 2. Perry-Castaneda Library. 3. Perry-Castaneda Library. 4. Perry-Castaneda Library. 5. Wikipedia. 6. Wikipedia. 7. Dr. William J. Ball, Department of Political Science, The College of New Jersey.

Melvil Dewey

1851–1931

Melvil Dewey

If it weren't for Melvil Dewey, finding a book in the library might be as frustrating as looking for a needle in a haystack. As a student at Amherst College, Melvil published a pamphlet that would totally change the way books are arranged on library shelves. For the first time, letters and numbers with decimals (now known as "call numbers") were assigned to books and other library materials, making it much easier to hunt down everything from the Nancy Drew and Hardy Boys mystery series to baseball statistics and presidential trivia. For librarians and library patrons everywhere, it's been the greatest invention since sliced bread.

The next time you visit a library, see if the book you are looking for is filed under the Dewey Decimal System. For example, does the call number 808.88 Col appear on the spine, or back, of the book called Six Sick Sheep: 101 Tongue Twisters? If it does, you may very well have Melvil Dewey to thank for making it so easy to find. He made today's library feel much like a big, walk-in computer. To use it, you only need to know the two most important things you learned in kindergarten: the alphabet and how to count.

Want to learn more about this father of library sciences? Visit http://tqjunior.thinkquest.org/5002, a Web site designed to teach kids about the Dewey Decimal System and the man who invented it. Or you can go to the library and look up more information about him beginning with the call number 020.92.

000 Generalities

Melville Louis Kossuth Dewey (that's a mouthful) was born into a very strict and thrifty family in upstate New York. His parents owned a store where they made and sold boots and shoes. They were "famous … for being the hardest working in town," and quite naturally they instilled a strong work ethic in each of their four children. Among their many chores, the Dewey kids tended cows, split wood, dug potholes, washed windows, spread ashes over the meadow, hauled gravel to the cemetery, carried goods to and from the train depot, helped out in their parents' store, and even cleaned their mother's sewing machine.

From a very early age, Melville enjoyed sorting and organizing things, including the kitchen pantry. An aunt recalled the boy's "mania for system and classification. It was his delight to arrange his mother's pantry, systematizing and classifying its contents." Melville's keen sense of order and logic showed up in his love of mathematics and earned him a reputation for being able to compute numbers in his head faster than his classmates could on paper. "He was like lightning in his calculations," one of his teachers remembered.

100 Philosophy

At age thirteen, Melville first showed his passion for books. So the story goes, he one day dropped into a bag all the coins he had earned helping with chores around the house, a total of about ten dollars in change. He then walked to a store about ten miles away to purchase the one thing he wanted more than anything in the world. The prized possession? Webster's unabridged dictionary. No kidding. Thirteen-year-old Melville walked ten miles and spent his entire life's savings on a dictionary!

> For Melville, this was the first of many dictionaries to come. He always had several dictionaries scattered around his house, so he could jump up from any reading chair and quickly look up a word's meaning. When he later became a teacher, he loved dictionaries so much he gave them as gifts to his students. Okay, okay. It's the thought that counts.

After buying the dictionary, Melville faced a major hurdle: the book was too heavy to carry home. So Melville forked over thirty cents, a whopping amount at the time, to buy a train ticket to transport his heavy load home. It proved to be a labor of love. Some sixty years later the memory of the treasured dictionary was still fresh in his mind. "At last I had the most essential book," he exclaimed.

200 Religion

Like most teenagers growing up in upstate New York, Melville skated in the winter and played ball, hiked, hunted, and fished in the summer. Unlike most teenagers, he also spent his free time lying face down on the carpet and reading. A journal he started keeping when he turned fifteen includes these juicy excerpts: "reading Macaulay's *History of England*—I like it very much" or "I staid with Wayne last night … reading poetry" or "reading Abercrombie's *Intellectual Philosophy*." Melville admitted that the books were sometimes way above his reading level, yet he tackled them anyway. "Be not afraid of hard study," he wrote. "It is the price of learning."

300 Social Sciences

In his journal, Melville didn't just reflect upon books he had read. He also examined himself, right down to the minutest detail. On his fifteenth birthday, he wrote:

> *I have been weighing and measuring myself this afternoon and find that I weigh one hundred twenty-five pounds and am five feet and five and a fourth inches in height. In looking over my stock of worldly goods I find that I have fifty dollars' worth of clothing, fifty dollars' worth of books, and twenty-five dollars' worth of miscellaneous traps.*

For the next ten years, on each of his birthdays, Melville made similar entries in his journal. And with each passing year, he became more and more frustrated that his growth, in inches and income, wasn't faster. He wrote: "Tomorrow I complete my eighteenth year and have accomplished during these eighteen years what I hope my children, if I ever have any (and not only hope but expect) will accomplish better in fifteen or less."

400 Languages

To accomplish more in life Melville decided to rid himself of bad habits, especially those habits that wasted time. He settled on *Reform* (the cleansing of an evil or wrong) as his life's work and bought a pair of cufflinks inscribed with the letter *R* as "a constant reminder … that I was to give my life to reforming certain mistakes and abuses."

What bad habits did Melville decide to drop? For one thing, he hated to waste time and energy writing extra letters in words. "Speling skolars agree that we hav the most unsyentifik, unskolarli, illojikal & wasteful speling ani languaj ever ataind," he boldly asserted. When he later became a member of Andrew Carnegie's Simplified Spelling Board, he suggested that school be spelled *skool*; honey as *huni*; and through as *thru*. Melville Louis Kossuth Dewey even tried to save time writing his own name. He first dropped his two middle names—*Louis* and *Kossuth*. Next, he omitted the *le* of Melville and, for a while, shortened *Dewey* to *Dui*. He finally settled on Melvil Dewey, the version for which he is now known worldwide.

500 Pure Sciences

Melvil was equally passionate about smoking being a waste of time and money. When he was sixteen he wrote an essay on the cost of smoking, noting that a man who smokes just one cigar a day, for fifty years, "has blown away in smoke what, with its interest, would have amounted to $14,794.50." (That was then. But if you were to smoke one pack of cigarettes a day for fifty years beginning *today*, you'd blow away a whopping $144,000.) With great foresight, he was also very concerned about the health risks of smoking. "Certainly God never made an animal with a natural desire to convert his mouth into a smokestack," he argued. We now know that such a smokestack causes lung cancer, heart disease, emphysema, and other respiratory problems.

> Over the years, Melvil urged other reforms. He was a huge fan of the metric system of weights and measures (for its simplicity); the banning of alcohol (which he disliked as much as cigarettes); and a form of writing known as shorthand (which saves time by using abbreviations and symbols for letters and words).

600 Applied Science and Technology

Seventeen-year-old Melvil's desire to change things was further "ignited" one frigid January day when a fire broke out in his classroom. He tried to save as many books as he could from the fire, but in the process he inhaled a great deal of smoke. (In the Extension Activities, read about Alia Muhammad Baker's more recent book rescue mission in Basra, Iraq.) Then, as the school building burned to the ground, Melvil stood outside in the cold with little clothing and watched the entire disaster unfold. Within a week, he had a deep and persistent cough, and a doctor predicted Melvil would not live more than a year or two.

The long illness proved to be a watershed in Melvil's life. With a heightened sense of his own mortality, he decided to make the most of his limited time on earth. Efficiency became his obsession, and he returned to his lifework, *Reform*, with added gusto. This time, all his energies were devoted to books.

700 Arts

By now a student at Amherst College, Melvil got a job at the library to help pay for his education. There, he saw room after room filled with stacks and stacks of books in total disarray. The books were horribly arranged, sometimes by size, sometimes by the author's last name, sometimes by the date the book was published, and sometimes even by color (so that a shelf would "look nice").

In other libraries Melvil visited, the system was no better. Books were often assigned a fixed spot on a shelf, and their corresponding location was recorded in the card catalog. The problem with this "fixed location" approach was that each time new acquisitions were added to a shelf, other books were pushed down or completely pushed off—meaning that all relevant catalog records had to be revised. "I was astounded to find the lack of efficiency, and waste of time and money" in running a library, Melvil candidly observed.

Now, this was all very upsetting to Melvil, especially when he was wasting hours and sometimes even days hunting down a single book. Given the importance of research in a college setting, he thought that the process of finding a book in the library should be absolutely quick and simple. The ability to read and "get the meaning from the printed page" was the "ultimate cornerstone of education," he reasoned.

Out of this frustration, reform-minded Melvil stumbled into his true calling. "For months I dreamed day and night that there must be somewhere a satisfactory solution," Melvil mused. He read hundreds of books, visited some fifty libraries, and talked to dozens and dozens of librarians. On his twenty-first birthday, he explained his obsession with this entry in his notebook: "The free school and the free library I conceive to be the great engines [of change]. I feel thankful for the strong interest in the work that has come to me during the last year … My World Work—Free Schools and Free Libraries for every soul."

As luck would have it, one day Melvil "blundered on" a pamphlet written by Nathaniel Shurtleff called *A Decimal System for the Arrangement and Administration of Libraries in the Amherst Library*. For most of us, the book would make our eyes glaze over. But not Melvil. He excitedly checked it out for, in his words, "my heart is open to anything that's either decimal or about libraries." Thanks to that open heart, Melvil came up with the single idea for which he is now most famous.

800 Literature

One Sunday morning, while daydreaming during a long and dull sermon in church, Melvil suddenly had a stroke of genius. He wrote (using simplified spelling):

> *While I lookt stedfastly at [the minister] without hearing a word, my mind absorbd in the vital problem, the solution flasht over me so that I jumpt in my seat and came very near shouting, 'Eureka' Use decimals to number a classification of all human knowledge in print.*

From *Readers and Leaders* by Susan Steffensen Romaine. Westport, CT: Libraries Unlimited.
Copyright © 2007 Libraries Unlimited.

Melvil's brainstorm was to assign "addresses" to books sitting on library shelves in the form of letters and numbers with decimals (now known as call numbers). Decimal, of course, refers to a numbering system based on ten. So Melvil's idea was to first divide all books into ten major categories—religion, philosophy, history, language, science, geography, and so on. Each of these categories was then split into ten categories, then split again into ten categories, then split again into ten categories—each time bringing more and more precision to a book's specific location on a shelf. For example, a book about Golden Retrievers would be classified like this:

600 Applied Science and Technology
  630 Agriculture & Related Technologies
    636 Animal Husbandry
      636.7 Dogs
        636.75 Golden Retrievers

Melvil later published his idea, combining his zeal for mathematics and orderliness, in a forty-two-page pamphlet called *A Classification and Subject Index for Cataloguing and Arranging the Books and Pamphlets of a Library*. Now known as the Dewey Decimal System, it not only brought order to the madness at Amherst University but quickly spread to libraries all over the country. Today almost every public and school library in the nation uses the Dewey Decimal System. Check out yours. What's more, the Dewey Decimal System has been translated into more than thirty languages and is now used in some 135 countries around the world. Even the World Wide Web uses the Dewey Decimal System to organize its googles and googles of information.

900 Geography and History

For librarians and library patrons everywhere, perhaps the true genius behind the Dewey Decimal System is its ability to accommodate the explosion of information since Melvil's day. All it takes is dividing Melvil's original categories into smaller and smaller gradations by adding more and more digits to the right of the decimal point. (For example, a book called *Valley Forge* by Richard Ammon has the call number J973.3341 Amm.) In such a simple yet mind-boggling way, Melvil's system not only classifies all the human knowledge that ever was, but all the information that ever will be. What a legacy for this zealot of order and logic!

Even Melvil was awed by his plan's flexibility in an ever-changing world. He wrote: "The system is easily understood and applies equally well to a library of a hundred volumes, or of a million, it being capable of indefinite and accurate growth; the system growing with the books in the same direction and at the same rate, an exceedingly desirable thing, wholly unattainable by any other plan yet proposed."

While Melvil is best remembered for the Dewey Decimal System, he made other lasting contributions to libraries. He published the first library journal, which included book reviews and new trends in library sciences. At the then all-male Columbia College (now coed Columbia University), he hired the first female librarians and opened the nation's first school of library science. He founded the American Library Association, which today represents thousands and thousands of librarians all over the country. And to earn a few dollars he formed a company called the Library Bureau, which originally furnished "libraries with equipment and supplies of unvarying correctness and reliability" and over the years has grown into the nation's leading manufacturer of library furniture. With that kind of resume, no wonder Melvil Dewey is widely recognized as the "Father of Modern Librarianship."

It was once said of Melvil: "Books were for him the tools—the essential tools—with which man might build for himself a better world." Today readers everywhere are reaping the benefits of his vision.

From *Readers and Leaders* by Susan Steffensen Romaine. Westport, CT: Libraries Unlimited.
Copyright © 2007 Libraries Unlimited.

Going the Extra Mile:
Extension Activities for Melvil Dewey

I. The Librarian of Basra

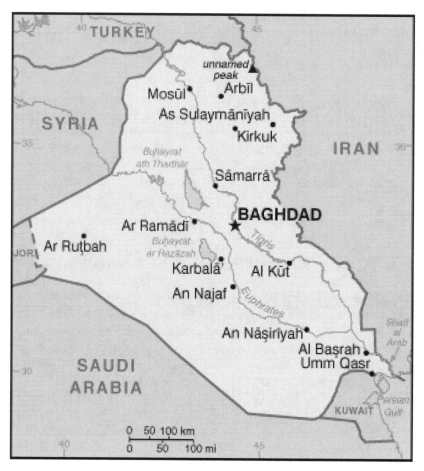

Map of Iraq

As a young girl living in Iraq, Alia Muhammad Baker loved to read books. She read about the history of her native country and its tribes and civilizations going back thousands of years. Of special interest was the invasion of Iraq by the Mongols in the thirteenth century, when the Great Baghdad Library was burned to the ground and many of its books were lost forever. According to Iraqi legend, so many books were flung into the Tigris during the invasion that the river ran blue from ink. Why would anyone want to destroy a library? Alia wondered.

Years later Alia found out, as chief librarian of the Central Library in Basra (shown on the map as the port of Al Basrah). With war breaking out in Iraq in 2003, Alia Muhammad Baker rescued nearly 30,000 books and ancient manuscripts from the Basra Central Library. She smuggled the "the past, present, and future of her country" right out from under the noses of soldiers occupying the library—just days before bombs rained down and the building was burned to the ground. "In the Koran, the first thing God said to

Muhammad was *Read*," Alia explained as her motivation. Still, the risks were formidable. Had Alia been caught smuggling the books, she would have been imprisoned for years or perhaps even put to death.

Where exactly did Alia store the 30,000 rescued books? Why, in her home, of course. With the help of dozens of friends, Alia filled her rooms to the rafters until a more permanent home could be found. "There are books in stacks, books in the cupboards, books bundled in the flour sacks like lumpy aid rations," she said of her living quarters. "Books fill an old refrigerator. Pull aside a window curtain, and there is no view, just more books."

Alia's story was first revealed to the world by *New York Times* reporter Shaila K. Dewan in an article titled, "Books Spirited to Safety before Iraq Library Fire." The article can be found at http://cpprot.te.verweg.com/2003-August/000226.html. Since its publication, people everywhere have been captivated by Alia's courageous rescue mission, including children's writer and illustrator Jeanette Winter. "I knew immediately that I needed to make a book out of this story," said Winter. "It was perfect."

From Winter's brainstorm came *The Librarian of Basra: A True Story from Iraq*. See if a copy sits on a shelf in your school library. If not, perhaps your class could purchase the book for your library's collection. Adding to the pleasure, a portion of the proceeds from the sale of each book goes toward the purchase of new books for the Basra Central Library's collection.

Of course, you can also send a check (made out to the American Library Association and marked "Iraq Book Program") to: International Relations Office, American Library Association, 50 E. Huron, Chicago, IL 60611. One donation, like one person, can truly make a difference.

II. The Library Hotel

Never in Melvil's wildest dreams would he have guessed that one day a luxury hotel would be built in Manhattan, overlooking the New York Public Library, based on his Dewey Decimal System. The Library Hotel is set up something like your local library. Each of the ten floors of the hotel has a general theme (religion, literature, philosophy, arts) and each of the sixty rooms is numbered like the Dewey Decimal System. For example, just as the 700s in the library are devoted to the arts, on the seventh floor of the hotel guests may stay in an architecture, painting or music room. Young children prefer the dinosaur room (500.005) or the fairy-tales room (800.005) on the fifth and eighth floors, respectively. The rooms are all lined with books and decorated with artwork exploring the Dewey Decimal System theme, while the Winnie the Pooh, Harry Potter, and Madeline rooms even come with matching bed sheets. Sound fun?

Adding to its charm, the hotel has a mahogany-paneled writer's den with a fireplace—a cozy spot to cuddle up with a good book. For those who prefer an outdoor hideaway, there is a quiet poetry garden. A handsome-looking card catalog in the lobby of the hotel lists the six thousand books and one hundred films that can be checked out and enjoyed by hotel patrons.

As a final "library touch," Belgian chocolates are left on the hotel room pillows at night, each with an inspiring message tucked inside. "When I step into this library, I cannot understand why I ever step out," reads one; and "I have always imagined that paradise will be a kind of library," reads another.

Now it's your turn to be an interior decorator. Design your own room at the Library Hotel, including everything from books and artwork to bed sheets and towels, all tied around the theme of your Dewey Decimal System room number. (To see the Dewey Decimal System in its entirety, visit http://www.ipl.org/div/teen/aplus/dewey1.htm.) It may be fun to coordinate wallpaper with your theme, as well as curtains and carpeting. You can even think about special messages wrapped in *your* Belgian chocolates and left on the pillow each night. Be creative … and sweet dreams.

III. Preserving a Newspaper Clipping (from November 1983 issue of *Cobblestone* magazine)

Have you ever clipped out a newspaper article to include in a scrapbook or diary? If so, you may have been surprised to discover just a few months later that the newspaper clipping had turned yellow and brittle. What causes the damage? For one thing, chemicals in the paper combine with moisture in the air to make sulphuric acid, which breaks apart the newspaper's fibers and causes it to crumble. Books are prone to the same aging process.

Unfortunately, acid is only one of paper's enemies. Others include light, especially ultraviolet rays, which bleaches paper and fades the print; molds and fungi that grow in between the pages of books and newspapers stored in damp places; and insects that discover crumbs of food left behind in the spine of books and then just keep nibbling away. Yes, there really are bookworms!

To better preserve their collections, librarians are now urging book and newspaper publishers to use acid-free paper that some say could last as long as four hundred to five hundred years. At the same time, more and more acid-free folders and boxes are being used to store books and newspaper in libraries. Here's something you can do right at home to preserve newspaper clippings using easy-to-find and inexpensive materials. Try it!

You need: a newspaper clipping, a milk of magnesia tablet, one quart of club soda, a flat pan (large enough to hold clipping), a piece of nylon mesh material (such as an old nylon stocking towel), and weights (such as paperweights or small stones).

1. Dissolve the milk of magnesia tablet in the club soda overnight.

2. Place the nylon mesh in the bottom of the pan and pour in the liquid.

3. Put the clipping on top of the mesh and soak it for about an hour.

4. Carefully remove the clipping from the pan. Use the mesh so you don't have to touch the wet paper.

5. Use towel to pat dry the clipping. Do not move clipping!

6. When clipping is partially dry, place weights on the corners to keep it from curling. Do not move clipping until it is completely dry.

7. Presto, you should have a well-preserved newspaper clipping to enjoy for many years to come.

From *Readers and Leaders* by Susan Steffensen Romaine. Westport, CT: Libraries Unlimited. Copyright © 2007 Libraries Unlimited.

References

Books, Magazines, and Newspapers

Denotes books and magazines of special interest to middle readers.

†*Denotes sources for quotations in this chapter.*

* † Corsey, Mark, ed. *Cobblestone's Checking Out Libraries.* Peterborough, NH: Cobblestone, November 1983 issue.

* † Dewan, Shaila K. "Books Spirited to Safety before Iraq Library Fire," *New York Times,* August 3, 2003.

* † Weber, Sandra. *"Eureka!" Dewey Did It: His System Helps You Every Time You Go to the Library (Melvil Dewey's Classification System for Books).* From *Highlights for Children Magazine,* October 1, 2002.

† Wiegand, Wayne A. *Irrepressible Reformer: A Biography of Melvil Dewey.* Chicago: American Library Association, 1996.

Websites

Melvil Dewey: The Father of Librarianship: www.booktalking.net/books/dewey.

Melvil Dewey's Obituary in the New York Times (dated December 27, 1931): www.nytimes.com/learning/general/onthisday/bday/1210.html.

Answers.com: www.answers.com/topic/melvil-dewey.

The Library Hotel: www.libraryhotel.com.

Additional Resources

Books

Cleary, Florence Damon. *Discovering Books and Libraries: A Handbook for Students in the Middle and Upper Grades.* New York: HW Wilson, 1976. A guide to libraries along with a detailed explanation on how to use reference materials. Each chapter concludes with a summary, quiz, and list of special projects.

Lipson, Eden Ross. *The New York Times Parent's Guide to the Best Books for Children: 3rd Edition, Revised and Updated.* New York: Three Rivers Press, 2000. This book cites the top one thousand children's books of the twentieth century. Titles include middle reading classics such as E. B. White's *Charlotte's Web* and Roald Dahl's *Charlie and the Chocolate Factory,* as well as young adult books such as S. E. Hinton's *The Outsiders* and Walter Dean Myer's *Scorpion.*

Miller, William. *Richard Wright and the Library Card.* New York: Lee & Low. This book is based on a scene from Richard Wright's autobiography, *Black Boy.* While Wright was working for an optical company in Memphis, he gained access to the public library with the help of a coworker—later inspiring him to become an internationally acclaimed writer.

Vahn, Sarah. *Melvil Dewey: His Enduring Presence in Librarianship*. Littleton: Libraries Unlimited, 1978. A well-written biography of Melvil Dewey with many family photographs.

Web Sites

Quotations about Librarians and Libraries: http://www.ifla.org/I/humour/subj.htm.

New York Times article (dated March 12, 1906): *Announcing the Creation of the Simplified Spelling Board:* http://www.twainquotes.com/19060312.html.

Places to Visit

Library of Congress in Washington, D.C. This library was originally founded in 1800 to ensure members of Congress were well-informed in making legislative decisions. It has since grown into the nation's largest library, housing every single book registered for copyright in the United States.

Boston Public Library. This was the nation's first free, tax-supported library. It now has an indoor courtyard where patrons can bring a picnic lunch to enjoy while reading.

Folger Shakespeare Library in Washington, D.C. This library contains the world's largest collection of Shakespeare materials. A children's Shakespeare Festival is held every May, and the plays are performed by children attending public schools in the Washington, D.C., area.

New York Public Library. Thanks in part to a $5.2 million donation from Andrew Carnegie, the New York Public Library is now one of the nation's leading libraries. It is guarded by two sculpted lions nicknamed "Patience" and "Fortitude"—qualities that New Yorkers displayed in seeing themselves through the Great Depression.

Illustration Credits

In the order photos appear in this chapter: 1. Wikipedia. 2. About, Inc., part of the *New York Times*.

Helen Keller

1880–1968

Helen Keller and Anne Sullivan

Have you ever heard the expression, Where there's a will, there's a way? It means that if you want something badly enough, you will figure out how to get it. There is no better person to exemplify this expression than Helen Keller. Even though she became blind and deaf when she was just a year and a half old, Helen wanted to read more than anything else in the world. She worked tirelessly, and, with the help of her longtime teacher, Annie Sullivan, one day her dream of reading on her own was realized. Helen learned to read Braille, first in English and later in French, German, and Latin, gently skimming her nimble fingers over page after page of raised dots. And once she learned to read, she never looked back. Books became Helen's lifelong passion.

*Spirited and determined as she was, Helen was not content to simply read books. She wanted more out of life. She became the first blind-deaf person to graduate from an American college, Radcliffe. She authored nineteen books, one of which became an international bestseller and is now widely regarded as one of the most important books of the twentieth century—*The Story of My Life.* Read it someday. She starred in a movie about her life,* Helen Keller in Her Story, *which won an Academy Award. She traveled to forty nations to champion the rights of the blind and deaf, enlisting the support of presidents, emperors, kings and queens, writers, inventors, and movie stars along the way. Indeed, Helen's life story has served as an inspiration to millions of people around the world, past and present.*

Today Helen remains one of America's greatest heroines. She is featured on Alabama's state quarter and her statue is included in the Statuary Hall of the United States Capitol. Let Helen's life be an inspiration to you, too. "If I, deaf, blind, find life rich and interesting," she challenged us, "how much more can you gain by the use of your five senses?"

When one door of happiness closes, another opens; but often we look so long at the closed door that we do not see the one which has been opened for us.

—Helen Keller

Helen Keller was born a happy, healthy baby in the sleepy little town of Tuscumbia, Alabama. The family's homestead, nicknamed Ivy Green for its walls crawling with thick ivy, was surrounded by a garden filled with vines of roses and tangled honeysuckle. It was in that lovely, fragrant garden that Helen's "miracle" would later occur.

Although Tuscumbia was slow-paced, Helen's home life bustled with activity. Her father, known as "the Captain," ran the local newspaper and often brought a journalist friend home for dinner. Nothing made the Captain happier than regaling his dinner guests with colorful stories about the battles he had fought during the Civil War.

Helen's mother, Kate, helped out on the family's plantation by growing vegetables and tending to the animals. In between chores she doted on Helen. "The beginning of my life was simple and much like every other little life," Helen later wrote. "I came, I saw, I conquered, as the first baby in the family always does."

Many considered the Kellers to be the most favored family in town right up until the day when nineteen-month-old Helen suddenly became sick with a high fever, a bad headache, and a stiff neck. Helen's doctor diagnosed "acute congestion of the brain and stomach" (now believed to have been scarlet fever) and told her parents she would not survive her illness.

Helen defied her prognosis, as she would the many naysayers later in her life. Just as suddenly as her fever appeared, it faded—but not without taking a huge toll. The first signs were that Helen slept poorly, tossing and turning all night. Later, when her name was called or the dinner bell rang, she no longer responded. In addition, her eyes never seemed to close, even when a hand moved close or the sunlight streamed on her face. Helen's mother and father soon realized the horrific truth: her high fever had closed Helen's eyes and ears forever.

"I was too young to realize what had happened," Helen wrote years later. "When I awoke and found that all was dark and still, I suppose I thought it was night, and I must have wondered why the day was so long coming. Gradually, however, I got used to the silence and darkness that surrounded me and forgot that it had ever been day."

Although the world is full of suffering, it is also full of the overcoming of it.

—Helen Keller

Helen was now "a child of the silent night." To put yourself in her shoes, try donning a blindfold and earplugs for a day. You would not be able to see the faces of family and friends, the world outdoors, the sunrise, the moon, books, the blackboard, the television screen, or the furniture you keep bumping into. Nor would you be able to hear friends laughing, CDs playing, birds chirping and dogs barking, the school bell ringing, or the wind whistling. You would not even be able to see yourself in the mirror or hear your own voice.

But lucky for you, when the day is over you would be able to remove the blindfold and the earplugs and your life would return to normal. Sadly, Helen was forever cut off from the world as she knew it. "Blindness separates people from things," Helen would later say. "Deafness separates people from people."

Helen's inability to communicate with family and friends became increasingly frustrating. "Sometimes I stood between two persons who were conversing and touched their lips," she later wrote. "I could not understand, and was vexed. I moved my lips and gesticulated frantically without result. This made me so angry at times that I kicked and screamed until I was exhausted."

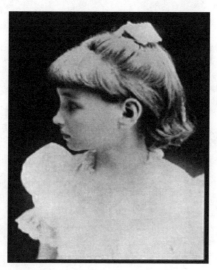

Helen Keller at age seven

Relatives soon lost all patience with Helen, calling her "a monster" or a "wild, destructive little animal." An uncle thought she was "mentally defective," suggesting she be sent away to a school for the deaf and blind, or a hospital for the mentally ill. Helen's parents agreed they needed to seek help—*pronto*—but secretly wondered if there was anyone out there who could really reach Helen.

Keep your face to the sunshine and you cannot see the shadow. It's what sunflowers do.

—Helen Keller

The Kellers spared no expense taking Helen to every doctor they could find for treatments ranging from mineral water spas to special electric tests. Sadly, none of the treatments worked; and none of the doctors even offered hope.

Then there was the Alabama Institute for the Deaf and Blind, a boarding school one hundred miles away from Tuscumbia. At first brush, it sounded perfect. Still, Helen's parents couldn't bear the thought of sending her away. Essentially a vocational school, students attending the Alabama Institute for the Deaf and Blind learned little more than to craft brooms, baskets, or chairs.

Worse yet was the thought of sending Helen to an asylum, which at the time housed the blind and deaf together with "the insane, the feeble-minded, the epileptic … the shiftless, the vicious, [the] respectable homeless." While Helen's parents agreed their daughter was almost impossible to raise on their own, they were equally certain an asylum was not the place for her.

Charles Dickens

Just when their situation appeared to be utterly hopeless, Helen's mother picked up a dog-eared copy of a forty-year-old book by the English writer Charles Dickens called *American Notes*. Life for the Kellers, and especially for Helen, would never be the same again.

Walking with a friend in the dark is better than walking alone in the light.

—Helen Keller

Kate pored over *American Notes*. In it, Charles Dickens wrote about visiting the Perkins Institution, the nation's very first school for the blind located in Boston, Massachusetts, and meeting a young girl named Laura Bridgman. Like Helen, Laura had become blind and deaf as a child, yet she had miraculously learned to communicate through something called finger spelling. (See "Finger Spelling" in the Extension Activities.)

With finger spelling, each letter of the alphabet is shown by a different hand position—much like sign language. But since Laura could not see the signs, they were painstakingly spelled into the palm of her hand so she could "feel" them. Through tireless determination, it worked. Laura went on to become the very first deaf and blind person to learn language and to communicate with the world around her.

Kate wondered, *If Laura Bridgman could communicate, then why not Helen? Wasn't there someone—anyone—at the Perkins Institution who could teach finger spelling to Helen?* Kate decided to make one more trip, this time to the Perkins Institution. Her perseverance paid off. Kate not only found a teacher for Helen, she found the perfect teacher. An A+ teacher, if you will. Anne Mansfield Sullivan was her name, but most people called her Annie.

As a child, Annie had been almost completely blind. Luckily, several operations helped her to regain her sight, although her eyes were never again normal. Annie went on to attend the Perkins Institution, where she graduated at the top of her class. That's when this smart and tough go-getter nicknamed "Miss Spitfire" learned that the Kellers were looking for a tutor to move to Tuscumbia to teach their blind and deaf daughter how to read, write, and communicate. Although Annie had no training, no special skills, and no experience for the job, she "seized upon the first opportunity that offered itself."

My birthday can never mean as much to me as the arrival of Annie Sullivan … That was my soul's birthday.

—Helen Keller

Annie's arrival at Ivy Green didn't exactly start off on the right foot. "I remember how disappointed I was when the untamed little creature stubbornly refused to kiss me and struggled to free herself from my embrace."

Annie knew right away that before she could teach, she must tame. "Obedience is the gateway through which knowledge and love enter the mind of the child," Annie explained. She first taught Helen how to sit properly at a dinner table, keeping her hands on her *own* food. She then taught her how to eat with a knife, fork, and spoon, and to use a napkin. She taught Helen to dress herself and to brush her hair. She even taught her how to control her temper. When Helen hit Annie, Annie hit Helen right back; when Helen pinched, shoved, or bit, Annie pinched, shoved, or bit right back. "Fortunately for us both, I am a little stronger, and quite as obstinate when I set out," Annie wrote.

It took a few scratches and bruises but progress finally came. "The wild creature … has been transformed into a gentle child," Annie noted. "It now remains my pleasant task to mold and direct the beautiful soul that is beginning to stir." In other words, Helen's *real* education was about to begin.

One can never consent to creep when one feels an impulse to soar.

—Helen Keller

Helen's *real* education was all about learning language. For the first lesson, Annie cradled one of Helen's hands and finger spelled the letters *d-o-l-l* into her palm. She then placed a doll in Helen's other hand, a special doll that students at the Perkins Institution had made just for Helen. Letters, then doll—a simple routine to help Helen make the connection between words and things. Annie repeated the lesson over and over, first fingering the letters in Helen's palm and then having her student brush her hand over the doll's face and through its hair.

The second word on Annie's list was *cake*. Good choice. A tasty way to attach meaning to a word. Annie first finger spelled the letters *c-a-k-e* into the palm of Helen's hand, and then gave her a piece of cake to nibble on. "I gave her the cake, which she ate in a great hurry," wrote Annie, "thinking I suppose that I might take it from her." With the next word, *bread*, Annie followed the same routine. Spelling, then tasting; words, then meanings.

Progress came at a snail's pace. Yes, Helen soon memorized Annie's finger movements, spelling out the words *doll, cake,* and *bread*, as well as *milk* and *mug* into Annie's hand. Helen even tried spelling into her dog's paw! Yet the eager student still didn't have a clue as to what Annie was really trying to teach her. *B-r-e-a-d* was just a series of letters to Helen, not a baked good. Nor did Helen make the connection between the letters in *c-a-k-e* and the sweet taste in her mouth. "I did not know that I was spelling a word or that words even existed," Helen would later remember. "I was simply making my fingers move in monkey-like imitation."

When we do the best that we can, we never know what miracle is wrought in our life, or in the life of another.

—Helen Keller

Then, one beautiful spring day, beside a water pump in the gardens of Ivy Green, what can only be considered a miracle suddenly occurred. As Annie pumped water and let it spill over Helen's fingers, she finger spelled w-a-t-e-r into Helen's palm. Helen's eyes brightened. Quickly, Annie did it again, pumping water then finger spelling the letters, w-a-t-e-r. Helen's entire face lit up. For the first time, Helen understood that the things she touched had a name and could be communicated. The cold, wet, gurgling stuff was the same thing as the letters w-a-t-e-r being spelled into the palm of her hand. Helen later described the life-altering moment in her autobiography:

> Suddenly I felt a misty consciousness as of something forgotten—a thrill of returning thought; and somehow the mystery of language was revealed to me. I knew then that "w-a-t-e-r" meant the wonderful cool something that was flowing over my hand. That living word awakened my soul, gave it light, hope, joy, set it free! There were barriers still, it is true, but barriers that could in time be swept away. I left the wellhouse eager to learn. Everything had a name, and each name gave birth to a new thought. As we returned to the house every object which I touched seemed to quiver with life.

Helen dropped to her knees, touched the ground, and eagerly asked for its name. *D-i-r-t*, spelled Annie. Helen then pointed to the water pump and asked for its name. *P-u-m-p*, spelled Annie. Then she pointed to herself. *H-e-l-e-n*, spelled Annie. Suddenly, Helen turned around and pointed to Annie. *T-e-a-c-h-e-r*, Annie spelled into her hand. That would be the name Helen would call Annie for the rest of her life.

Helen went on to learn some thirty new words that day, as Annie's fingers danced across her curious little palm. Helen later wrote: "It would have been difficult to find a happier child than I was as I lay in my crib at the close of that eventful day and lived over the joys it had brought me, and for the first time longed for a new day to come."

The best and most beautiful things in the world cannot be seen or even touched. They must be felt within the heart.

—Helen Keller

Out of the blue, a whole new world opened up to Helen. "I did nothing but explore with my hands and learn the name of every object that I touched," she later wrote. Much of her exploring was outdoors, with Annie at her side, finger spelling word after word into her hand. "Our happiest school room was the roadside or a field or beside the Tennessee River," Annie recalled.

Helen felt the wind rustle the cornstalks. She cupped a baby chick and a butterfly in her hands. She let wriggling, slimy tadpoles slide between her fingers. She held crickets in her hand to "feel" their chirp. Why, she learned to tell the difference between a white and a purple lilac just from their shape and smell. Eventually, she even managed to walk to a riverbank and build a map of the world out of mud, rocks, sticks, leaves, bark, and grass. "All my early lessons have in them the breadth of the woods—the fine, resinous odor of pine needles, blended with the perfume of wild grapes," Helen wrote.

Then came the day when Helen learned an even deeper, richer lesson about words. It was the day she learned that some things can't be touched or felt or even sensed—abstract things. Helen asked Annie what *love* was. Well, her teacher explained, love was like the clouds that give rain and help flowers grow. The clouds themselves could not be touched, but you could feel the raindrops and smell the flowers that the clouds produced. Love was much the same. You couldn't touch it, but you could still feel how sweet it made the days feel. As Helen later realized, "The beautiful truth burst upon my mind—I felt that there were invisible lines stretched between my spirit and the spirit of others."

Louis Braille

We the blind are as indebted to Louis Braille as mankind is to Gutenberg.

—Helen Keller

Helen was now ready to take on the biggest challenge of her life. She could neither see nor hear words, but she was determined to read them.

Braille would be the answer to her prayers. Invented in France by Louis Braille, who was himself blinded in an accident at age three, Braille used different combinations of raised dots to represent the twenty-six letters of the alphabet. (See "Braille Alphabet" in the Extension Activities.) These dots were punched into paper with a special stylus (a sharp, hard-pointed pen-like instrument) to make them stand out on a page. That way, they could more easily be read or actually "felt" by a person who was blind.

Helen quickly mastered Braille and was soon reading books on her own. "No barrier of the senses shuts me out from … my book friends. They talk to me without embarrassment or awkwardness." Of course, Annie was determined that Helen read only good literature, "in all its power." Once when Annie caught Helen reading *The Last Days of Pompeii*, a trashy novel of its time, she was furious, pounding into her hand, "Caught, discovered, trapped!" It would be the classics or nothing, as far as Teacher was concerned.

After reading through all the Braille classics in Alabama, it soon became time to search for new books. Annie and Helen boarded a train for the Perkins Institution's Library in Boston, which housed the largest collection of Braille books in the world. Here, Helen felt much like the proverbial kid in a candy shop, pouncing upon books with raised-dot pages, one after another. Helen wrote of the books, "They tell me so much that is interesting about things I cannot see. And they are never troubled or tired like people."

In a word, literature is my utopia. Here I am not disenfranchised. No barrier of the senses shuts me out.

—Helen Keller

Always setting new goals for herself, Helen next decided to attend college. For three years, she worked hard to prepare for the college entrance exams, studying algebra, geometry, Greek and Roman history, German, French, Latin, and literature. It was during this time that her love of books deepened and she came to appreciate "an author, to recognize his style as I recognize the clasp of a friend's hand."

Among the writers Helen especially liked reading were philosophers such as Socrates, Plato, and Descartes, who "waked something in me that has never slept." She also delved into *The Iliad* and *The Odyssey*, *Little Lord Fauntleroy*, Charles Lamb's *Tales of Shakespeare*, the Bible, and the works of great American poets such as Henry Wadsworth Longfellow, John Greenleaf Whittier, and Oliver Wendell Holmes. To Annie's amazement, Helen "grasped the essentials of a narrative almost as quickly as I did, and her perception of beautiful words and images delighted me."

All of the hard work paid off as Helen was accepted into Radcliffe College, Harvard University's sister college for women at the time. "I knew there would be obstacles to conquer," Helen wrote, "but they only whetted my desire to try my strength by the standards of normal students."

Helen's words were prophetic, for college life was indeed tough. Annie finger spelled the key points of every course lecture into Helen's hands. And because most of the textbooks were not available in Braille, Annie painstakingly finger spelled Helen's reading assignments, too, which consumed as much as four to five hours a day.

It took a Herculean effort for Helen to keep up with her course work. While other students slept, Annie and Helen often studied together until the wee hours of the morning. At times, Annie grew tired from the strain, as the repetition of finger spelling gave her headaches and blurred vision. Helen worried that "she could not see much farther than the end of her nose" and that her "dear hand would not be equal to the task."

With so little time to enjoy the "lighter side" of college life, Helen and Annie naturally went through ups and downs, even some trials and tribulations, in their relationship. But in the end, they were always there for one another, urging the other on. The day of graduation, when Helen's name was called, *both* women walked gracefully across the stage. Helen's nimble fingers then reached out and grasped something no other deaf-blind person had ever earned—a college diploma. "The hilltop hour would not be half so wonderful if there were no dark valleys to traverse," exclaimed Helen.

We are never really happy until we try to brighten the lives of others.

——Helen Keller

After her graduation from Radcliffe, Helen discovered what would become her lifework: championing the rights of the blind. Working for the American Foundation for the Blind, she traveled around the world, making as many as five speeches a day and raising money for others living in darkness. Most of the funds she raised were devoted to taping "talking books" for the blind and to translating books into Braille, causes she cared for deeply. She also traveled to Washington, D.C., where she convinced

Congress to establish national public libraries for the blind, so that books in Braille would be more accessible to those who would benefit.

With the Foundation's backing, Helen assumed yet another role during World Wars I and II: she comforted wounded soldiers in military hospitals, especially those who had lost their eyesight or hearing. Life wasn't over, she reassured them. It would be forever different, but not over. Even if colorful blossoms could no longer be seen, their scents could still be savored. And even if musical notes could no longer be heard, their vibrations could still be felt. Don't wallow in your misfortune, Helen pleaded, but move on with your life. "Self-pity is our worst enemy and if we yield to it, we can never do anything good in the world," she cajoled.

Helen took up many other causes, some of which were quite daring at the time. Viewing herself as first and foremost "a human being with a mind of her own," she became a strong advocate of women's suffrage, or right to vote. She authored many articles calling for racial equality and world peace. She condemned poverty, convinced that our nation could do better taking care of its hungry, homeless, and unemployed. She spoke at rallies calling for shorter work days and better pay for women and children. As for the deplorable working conditions in cities all across the nation, she wrote: "I have visited sweatshops, factories, crowded slums. If I could not see [the filth], I could smell it."

Perhaps most importantly, Helen inspired millions of people with disabilities of their own to become meaningful and productive members of society. "While they were saying among themselves it cannot be done, it was done," Helen said about her own accomplishments. She urged others with disabilities to do the same.

Life is either a daring adventure or nothing.

—Helen Keller

As Helen grew old, she retreated into her comfortable home with her books. Annie had long since died, leaving a void in Helen's life that was never completely filled. One friend tried, however, reading twenty-two pages a day to Helen—the precise number of pages that Annie had read to Helen during their many years together.

A very spiritual woman, Helen's days often ended just as they began, by reading the scriptures. Through these readings, Helen no longer feared death. "What is so sweet as to awake from a troubled dream and behold a beloved face smiling upon you?" she once wrote. "I have to believe that such shall be our awakening from earth to heaven."

Helen also took pleasure in the writings of a philosopher named Emanuel Swedenborg, who believed in a heaven where everyone could see, hear, walk, and talk. It was a heaven where there were no disabilities or limitations. Comforted by Swedenborg's words, Helen later explained: "Death is no more than the passing from one room into another. But there's a difference for me, you know, because in that other room I shall be able to see."

Just weeks before her eighty-eighth birthday, Helen passed gently into the "other room." She died just as she had lived: a dignified and courageous human being. "The most pathetic person in the world is someone who has sight but has no vision," Helen once said. Although blind almost her entire life, Helen remains one of the great visionaries of our time.

Going the Extra Mile:
Extension Activities for Helen Keller

I. Finger Spelling

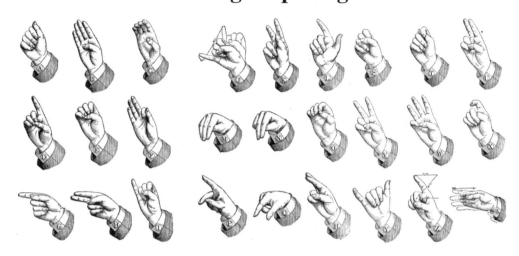

American finger alphabet

With finger spelling, each letter of the alphabet is shown by using a different hand position. With the letter *A*, for example, the hand is curled in a fist but with the thumb across the index finger at the end of the curl. Using the diagram, try to memorize the hand positions for *all* twenty-six letters of the alphabet. Some will come easily; others will take some effort.

Once you've mastered the finger alphabet, it's time to start actually using it. Here are just a few pointers on technique to keep in mind: go slowly at first—very slowly—and with a steady rhythm. Jerky and sloppy motions are difficult for others to read. Speed will come with practice. Note that double letters are shown by moving the hand to the side in a bumpy pattern, or by simply remaking the letter. To show the end of a word, pause by holding the letter for an extra beat of the spelling rhythm.

Begin by finger spelling your name. Next, finger spell the following words: *boy, girl, ear, nose, eat, cry, run, cat, dog, pot, hand, foot, zap, sun,* etc. Make up some additional words, but just be sure to keep the words to three or four letters at the start.

For a bigger challenge try finger spelling Helen's famous phrase, *Literature is my utopia*. As you do, remember to pause after each word so the letters don't all mesh together and the phrase can be more easily deciphered by others.

Now for the real test. Blindfold a friend, then try finger spelling a secret message into his or her hand. See if your blindfolded friend can decode the message. A slow and tedious means of communication? You betcha. But for Helen, this was her *only* form of communication.

II. Braille Alphabet

Blinded by an accident at age three, Louis Braille was determined to discover a new method of writing that would unlock the doors to literacy for himself and blind people everywhere. Here's the amazing story behind his invention of Braille:

In the early 1800s, Charles Barbier, a French army officer, invented a form of writing using dots and dashes punched into paper tape. Known as "Night Writing," it was intended to help soldiers communicate with each other on the battlefield in the dark hours of the evening.

When Louis Braille learned of "Night Writing," he realized it could be just as useful for the blind wishing to read as for soldiers hoping to communicate. Still, Barbier's system was overly complicated, thought Louis; it could take as many as fourteen dots and dashes to represent *each* letter and sound. That was way too many to feel with the fingertips at one time. What's more, Louis knew from his own experience that dots were much easier to feel than dashes.

So Louis got rid of the dashes and invented a remarkably simple Braille alphabet using just six dots, much like a domino. Depending on which of the six dots are raised—or darkened, in the table below—every single letter of the alphabet can be represented. For example, the letter *A* is shown by a raised dot in the upper left position; the letter *C,* by two raised dots in the top tier. Because of its simplicity, Braille is still used by the blind all over the world today.

Braille Alphabet

Unlike Barbier's system, Braille can also be written using punctuation marks, capital letters, contractions, and numbers. Visit http://www.afb.org/braillebug/braille_deciphering.asp to learn more about deciphering the Braille code. You can even send secret email messages in Braille by visiting http://www.afb.org/braillebug/emailmessage.asp. Check it out.

III. Learning to Live with Disabilities

Read William Gibson's *The Miracle Worker,* a three-act play about the physical and emotional challenges Helen Keller and Annie Sullivan faced together and ultimately overcame. It is considered one of the most moving accounts ever written of the will to succeed in the face of adversity. As you read it, think about disabled individuals that you know, people who are attending your school or living in your community. What are some of the obstacles they face, day in and day out? Make a list with some examples, whether it be finding reliable transportation to work or even just getting showered and dressed each morning. Then share your list with your classmates to better appreciate the full gamut of the challenges faced by many people who are disabled.

While the challenges must certainly feel overwhelming at times, fortunately there are all kinds of services and accommodations available through schools and local agencies to assist the disabled. For example, there are lifts in school buses and ramps built along staircases providing wheelchair accessibility; library books on tape or in large print to help the visually impaired; chrome plates with Braille posted inside public elevators and outside public restrooms; interpreters offering sign language at public addresses; and even smoke alarms that can be detected both visually and audibly.

By doing some investigative work, find out about some of the services and accommodations available at your school for students who are disabled. This may require interviewing a special education or special resources teacher, talking with students with various disabilities and learning about some of the services they receive through your school, touring both the inside and outside of your school and noting some of the special accommodations that are available in the classrooms and on the playground, and even reading about some of the special services your school is required to provide under the Americans with Disabilities Act or the bylaws of your school district.

Once you finish your research, summarize your findings using note cards and then prepare an oral presentation to your class. Keep in mind that you want to speak loudly and clearly so that your comments can be easily heard by *all* of your classmates.

References

Books and Magazines

Denotes books and magazines of special interest to middle readers.

†*Denotes sources for quotations in this chapter.*

* † Corsey, Mark, ed. *Cobblestone's Helen Keller/America's Disabled*. Peterborough, NH: Cobblestone Publishing, May 1983 issue.

* Freedman, Russell. *Out of Darkness: The Story of Louis Braille*. New York: Clarion Books, 1997.

* † Garrett, Leslie. *Helen Keller: A Photographic Story of a Life*. New York: DK Publishing, 2004.

* Gibson, William. *The Miracle Worker*. New York: Knopf, 1957.

Graff, Stewart, and Polly Anne Graff. *Helen Keller: Crusader for the Blind and Deaf*. New York: Bantam Doubleday Dell Books for Young Readers, 1965.

* † Keller, Helen. *The Story of My Life*. New York: H.W. Wilson, 1976 (reprint).

* Lawlor, Laurie. *Helen Keller: Rebellious Spirit*. New York: Holiday House, 2001.

Additional Resources

Web Sites

Famous Quotations of Helen Keller: www.quotationspage.com/quotes/helen_keller/.

Helen Keller Kids Museum: www.afd.org/braillebug/helen_keller_bio.asp. Read a kid-friendly biography about Helen, as well as some fun facts and inspiring quotes.

The My Hero Project: Annie Mansfield Sullivan: http://www.myhero.com/myhero/hero.asp?hero=a_sullivan. Find a biography about Helen's teacher and best friend, as well as related links and recommended readings.

Places to Visit

Gallaudet College in Washington, D.C. This one-hundred-acre campus is the site of the world's only liberal arts college for the deaf.

Ivy Green in Tuscumbia, Alabama. Visit Helen's childhood home where the water pump still stands in the backyard and many of the original furnishings are still intact. Nearby is the cottage where Annie Sullivan tutored Helen for many years.

Perkins School for the Blind in Watertown, Massachusetts. This school continues to house one of the largest collections of Braille books in the world.

Washington National Cathedral in Washington, D.C. Visit the tombs of Helen Keller and Annie Sullivan, which sit side-by-side in St. Joseph's Chapel.

Videos

The Miracle Worker. MGM Studio, 1962.

Illustration Credits

In the order photos appear in this chapter: 1. Wikipedia. 2. Wikipedia. 3. Wikipedia. 4. Wikimedia Commons. 5. Wikipedia.

Harry S Truman

1884 - 1972

Harry S Truman

You've studied Harry S Truman, right? In the history books, he's listed as the thirty-third President of the United States, although he always insisted he was just the thirty-second since Grover Cleveland served two nonconsecutive terms. Harry is perhaps best known for making the decision to drop the atomic bomb on Japan, precipitating the end to World War II. Yet there's also a lot of fun trivia about Harry you probably didn't know. For one thing, he almost always had his nose behind a book as a kid. He loved books so much that by the time he was just thirteen or fourteen years old, he had read every single book in his hometown library. Books were Harry's window to the world.

Harry was quite musical, too. Each morning he would arise at 5:00—that's right, 5:00 A.M.—to practice on the family's upright Kimball piano for two hours before school. Harry dreamed of becoming a concert pianist some day but had to settle instead for "tickling the ivories" while president. In fact, he brought three pianos with him to the White House and occasionally regaled guests with "The Missouri Waltz."

Harry's path to the presidency also makes for an interesting story. Most presidents got their start as lawyers, teachers, and farmers—but not Harry. He was the only president to begin his career as owner of a men's clothing store, otherwise known as a haberdasher. Truman & Jacobson sold everything from underwear to neckties. Although the store went through hard times and eventually could not pay its bills, Harry refused to declare bankruptcy. Instead, he repaid every penny of his share of the debt over the course of fifteen years.

Harry brought this same simple honesty and trustworthiness to the White House. When he wrote letters to his mother and sister, as he did almost every day, he always paid for the stamps with his own money. Even though special governmental privileges allowed presidents to send their mail free, Harry didn't even consider passing a personal expense—however small—along to the taxpayers.

There are lots of entertaining books about presidential trivia, but an especially good one is Lives of the Presidents: Fame, Shame (and What the Neighbors Thought) by Kathleen Krull. To borrow a haberdasher's phrase, it'll knock your socks off!

From *Readers and Leaders* by Susan Steffensen Romaine. Westport, CT: Libraries Unlimited.

Harry S Truman was born in Lamar, Missouri, a dusty, windblown town with an Old West flavor. Soon after his birth, Harry's father, a mule and horse trader, nailed a good-luck horseshoe above the front door of the family's small frame house. With horse trading slow and little money in the bank, the Trumans figured they needed all the good luck they could get.

Baby Harry was named after his uncle, Harrison Young. But the middle name was the intriguing one. Harry's parents couldn't decide between Shippe, in honor of one grandfather, and Solomon, in honor of the other. In the end, they compromised with the letter *S* which could stand for either Shippe or Solomon but actually stood for nothing. Harry Truman is the only president with a middle initial that doesn't represent a name.

> When swearing in the thirty-third president of the United States, Chief Justice Harlan Stone began, "I, Harry Shippe Truman ..." The soon-to-be-president quickly corrected him: "I, Harry S Truman, ... do solemnly swear that I will faithfully execute the office of the President of the United States ..."

Truman farm home in Grandview, Missouri

During his early years, Harry's family moved from one small Missouri town to another. The Trumans finally settled on a farm in Grandview, when Harry was three. The farmhouse may have been small but it came with lots of land—some six hundred acres, to be exact. It was the perfect place for Harry to ride his black Shetland pony, hunt for bird nests, gather wild strawberries, swing under an old shaded elm tree, and run in the prairie grass with his black-and-tan dog, Tandy, and his cat, Bob. "I just had the happiest childhood that could ever be imagined," Harry later said.

Just as the wide open space enraptured Harry, so, too, did all the boys and girls in the neighborhood who congregated at his house. Among them was a pretty girl with blue eyes, golden curls, and a big smile whom he had first met at his Presbyterian Sunday School. Her name was Elizabeth, but everyone called her Bess, for short. For Harry it was love at first sight, although he didn't exactly plunge into romance. After their first play date, when he was six and she was five, Harry felt so "backward" that he didn't talk to Bess for another five years, when he asked if he could carry her books home from school.

It wasn't until Harry was twenty-six years old that he wrote his first love letter to Bess, beginning one of the most eloquent collections of love letters ever written. If you would like to read some of them, visit the Web site "Dear Bess: Love Letters from the President" at www.trumanlibrary.org/dearbess.htm. And in case you're wondering, Harry and Bess finally tied the knot when he was thirty-five and she thirty-four years of age. During their White House years together, they remained the closest of friends. He often referred to her as "the Boss," seldom made a decision without first consulting her, and regarded her as a "full partner ... politically and otherwise."

No one in the world can take the place of your mother. Right or wrong, from her viewpoint you are always right. She may scold you for the little things, but never for the big ones.

—Harry Truman

Then there was Harry's incomparable mother, Martha, known as Matt or Mattie to her friends. Harry thought that she was smarter than just about anyone, and she seemed to understand him the best, too. She played the piano well, excelled in sports, and always spoke her mind—a trait she passed along to her son. It was Mattie who taught Harry to read when he was just five years old, holding him in her lap while pointing to the large letters in the family Bible.

A year later, however, Mattie began to wonder just how much Harry could actually see. He squinted when reading the smaller print in newspapers and magazines. Then, the night of a Fourth of July fireworks display, she noticed that Harry was far more interested in the sounds of the rockets than the lights in the sky. Putting two and two together, she realized that Harry was "blind as a mole."

Mattie quickly hitched up her horses and took Harry to an eye doctor in nearby Kansas City. He diagnosed "flat eyeballs," but the prognosis was not as bad as it sounded. Harry had hypermetropia, or farsightedness, meaning he could see objects far away but anything up close was blurry. The six-year-old was fitted with a pair of double-strength, wire-rimmed eyeglasses at a cost of $10—a lot of money in those days.

Harry wore glasses for the rest of his life, making him one of a dozen bespectacled presidents. The other presidents who either wore glasses or contact lenses were George Washington, Thomas Jefferson, Abe Lincoln, Theodore Roosevelt, Woodrow Wilson, Franklin Roosevelt, Dwight Eisenhower, Lyndon Johnson, Richard Nixon, Ronald Reagan, and George Herbert Walker Bush.

A pessimist is one who makes difficulties of his opportunities and an optimist is one who makes opportunities of his difficulties.

—Harry Truman

Wearing glasses for the first time can be a memorable experience for a kid. With thick, coke-bottle lenses, Harry suddenly looked very … well, nerdy. Worse, the glasses severely limited Harry's activities. For along with the prescription came a stern warning from his optometrist about the dangers of broken glass in his eye. "I was so carefully cautioned by the eye doctor about breaking my glasses and injuring my eyes," Harry wrote, "that I was afraid to join in the rough-and-tumble games in the school yard and back lot." He began to run away from playground scuffles and turn down invitations to play hockey, football, or baseball. Some of his classmates even started to call him "Four Eyes" and "Sissy."

Still, every cloud has a silver lining. "When I first put the glasses on I saw things and saw print I'd never seen before," Harry admitted. A whole new world of books, newspapers, and magazines suddenly opened up to him and carried him far beyond his boyhood home—a world that Harry's parents did their best to broaden.

Harry's parents may have been cash-strapped, but they wisely invested what little money they had in books. His father, for example, stashed loose change in a tray from an old steamer trunk until there was enough in savings to purchase a new book. This family book fund served its purpose because years later, Harry said that he could never recall being bored as a child, not once. "We always had a houseful of books," he explained.

Among Harry's favorite books was the family's "big old Bible" which he read three times, cover-to-cover. He also pored over Plutarch's *Lives* about the ancient Greeks and Romans, the complete set of William Shakespeare's plays, and Mark Twain's *The Adventures of Huckleberry Finn* and *Tom Sawyer*. All this reading was not something you talked about outside the house, Harry humbly noted. "It was just something you did."

Yet the rewards were plentiful. As a bright, curious, and diligent student, Harry liked school from the get-go. He liked his first-grade teacher. He liked his second-grade teacher. In fact, he liked *all* his teachers. "They were the salt of the earth," Harry later said, "and they gave us our high ideals."

Not surprisingly, Harry's grades were exemplary. On his second-grade report card, his scores were in the 90s in reading and spelling, and in language and mathematics he received a perfect 100. His lowest grade was an 86 in writing, but even with that there was a good explanation. Naturally left-handed, Harry was forced to learn to write with his right hand. He later went back to what felt natural, becoming one of seven presidents who were designated "South Paws."

> The other left-handed Presidents were James Garfield, Herbert Hoover, Gerald Ford, Ronald Reagan, George Herbert Walker Bush, and Bill Clinton. Actually, James Garfield was ambidextrous—he could use both hands equally well. He enjoyed dazzling people by writing in Latin with one hand and Greek with the other.

I studied the lives of great men and famous women, and I found that the men and women who got to the top were those who did the jobs they had in hand, with everything they had of energy and enthusiasm and hard work.

—Harry Truman

Truman home in Independence, Missouri

By now, Harry's family had moved to Independence, Missouri, the town he would call "home" for the rest of his life. Harry was reading, in his own words, "everything I could get my hands on—histories and encyclopedias and everything else."

For his tenth birthday, his mother gave him a four-volume set of large illustrated books called *Great Men and Famous Women*. The title may sound dry to some people, but Harry soaked up its contents like a sponge. He read and reread the hundreds of biographies comprising the set, enjoying the books so much that he later credited the gift with the beginning of his lifelong love of history.

As he read *Great Men and Famous Women,* Harry dreamed of becoming a great general himself one day and making history on the battlefield. He was most inspired by the famous warrior Hannibal, who had only one eye. "There is not in all history so wonderful an example of what a single man of genius may achieve against tremendous odds." Andrew Jackson also became a special hero of his: a man of action who was free-thinking and not at all stuck up. His other favorites were military leaders such as George Washington, Stonewall Jackson, Jeb Stuart, and his mother's idol, Robert E. Lee. It was to be worthy of her, Harry claimed, that he studied so many great men and events in history.

Not all readers become leaders. But all leaders must be readers.

—Harry Truman

Harry's fascination with books was fueled by the Independence Public Library. The town's library had two rooms with high ceilings, lined with more than two thousand books. It was topped by a white plaster bust of Benjamin Franklin. Harry visited the library just about every spare moment, devouring one book after another. "By the time I was thirteen or fourteen years old," he later wrote, "I had read all the books in the Independence Public Library." Even the encyclopedias! Harry later considered this to be the greatest accomplishment of his lifetime, although he also joked that he "had more useless information floating around in my head than any man."

From *Readers and Leaders* by Susan Steffensen Romaine. Westport, CT: Libraries Unlimited.
Copyright © 2007 Libraries Unlimited.

A bookish-looking Harry Truman

Of all the books in the library, Harry's favorites were about history and the people who made it. "Reading history, to me, was far more than a romantic adventure," he explained. "It was solid instruction and wise teaching which I somehow felt that I wanted and needed."

With all the information gleaned from reading history books, Harry was soon forming opinions that were not always consistent with those around him. Take Abraham Lincoln. Everyone in the Truman family despised the president. As Southerners, they simply could not forgive Lincoln for his position on slavery during the Civil War. But the more Harry read about Lincoln, the more he admired the president for his leadership in bringing two nations back together again as one, a viewpoint Harry was not shy about sharing with his family.

After graduating from high school, Harry hoped to study history at the University of Missouri and perhaps become a history teacher. But this part of his life did not go as planned. His father made some unwise business investments, leaving the family with no money to pay for college tuition. Harry's only hope for attending college was to gain appointment to the U.S. Military Academy at West Point, New York; but, unfortunately, he failed the physical exam due to his poor eyesight. So Harry instead went to work as a timekeeper for a railroad company, calling the job a "down to earth" education.

> Harry was one of nine presidents who never attended college—and the only one in the twentieth century. The other self-educated presidents were George Washington, Andrew Jackson, Martin Van Buren, Zachary Taylor, Millard Fillmore, Abraham Lincoln, Andrew Johnson, and Grover Cleveland.

From *Readers and Leaders* by Susan Steffensen Romaine. Westport, CT: Libraries Unlimited.

We can never tell what is in store for us.

—Harry Truman

President Franklin Delano Roosevelt

Little did Harry know that one day he'd grow up not just to read about history but to make history, too. When President Franklin Roosevelt died suddenly in office, Harry Truman, who had been vice president for just a few weeks and hardly even knew the president, became top dog. The world was at war, and here at home, the nation was engulfed in social and economic hardship. Enter Harry, in some ways the least likely of men to rule the most powerful nation on earth during its most perilous time in modern history. Speaking to reporters, Harry said, "Boys, if you ever pray, pray for me now. I don't know whether you fellows ever had a load of hay fall on you. But when they told me yesterday what had happened, I felt like the moon, the stars, and all the planets had just fallen on me."

As president, Harry stood five feet, eight inches tall. He had steely gray hair, wore wiry glasses with coke-bottle lenses, dressed in tailor-made suits with an American Legion button on the lapel, and usually topped off his outfit with a dapper hat. A man of simple routines, he ate the same breakfast every morning—juice, cereal, two pieces of whole wheat toast, and a glass of milk. (He was also known to sneak a glass of bourbon in the morning, for he believed it was good for his circulation.) Breakfast was always followed by a brisk walk, two miles at a clip of 128 steps a minute. His life was so common and so ordinary that some people said: "If Harry can be president, so could my next door neighbor."

Yet Harry's down-to-earth nature concealed his true greatness. Thanks to all the books he had read as a young boy, Harry had a penetrating mind that could sort through tons of information and form broad understandings of the great issues of the day. There was a full plate abroad: bringing an end to World War II, rebuilding Europe after the war through the Marshall Plan, and then maintaining world peace through new organizations such as the United Nations and the North Atlantic Treaty Organization. Here at home he faced stiff debate over civil rights, labor unions, and federal health insurance for the elderly. "I suppose considering the fact that I became President of the United States, reading was never time wasted," he deadpanned.

The Buck Stops Here.

—Harry Truman

The dropping of the bomb on Nagasaki

By far the gravest decision of Harry's presidency was one of his first: to drop atomic bombs on Japan, in the cities of Hiroshima and Nagasaki. The bombs brought about an abrupt end to World War II, perhaps saving millions of lives in the process. But in Harry's own words, the bombs also caused "a rain of ruin from the air the like of which has never been seen on this earth." To the end, Harry never doubted his decision. "The President—whoever he is—has to decide," Harry explained. "He can't pass the buck to anybody. No one else can do the deciding for him. That's his job."

> There's an interesting story behind the phrase, *Pass the Buck*. It originated with the game of poker, in which a marker or buck was used to show the player whose turn it was to deal. If a player chose not to deal, he or she could pass the buck to the next player. Over time, the expression came to mean one person passing a job or a responsibility onto someone else. As a reminder that it is ultimately the president's responsibility to make crucial decisions, Harry kept on his desk a plaque that read, *The Buck Stops Here*—and lived by its message by assuming full responsibility for all his decisions and actions. Today it is the slogan most often used in describing Harry Truman and explaining all the tough decisions he made as president.

For all the challenges he faced both at home and abroad, Harry still found time for relaxation. He spent much of his leisure time with his wife, Bess, and their daughter, Margaret—reading, listening to the radio, and playing the piano together. They enjoyed each other's company so much that the White House staff often referred to them as "the Three Musketeers." Of course, they were also quick to jump to each other's defense should the least bit of criticism be hurled. When Margaret performed her first vocal recital in Washington, D.C., for example, a scathing review appeared the next morning in the local newspaper. Harry was furious, dashing off a letter to the reviewer: "Some day I hope to meet you. When that happens you'll need a new nose [and] a lot of beefsteak for black eyes!"

Any man who has had the job I've had and didn't have a sense of humor wouldn't still be here.

—Harry Truman

Bess Truman

After leaving the White House, Harry and Bess moved back to the only home they had known all their married life—their stately Victorian home in Independence. A cartoon at the time showed a small boy wearing glasses and holding a book under his arm, walking beside a friend who is saying, "O.K., so you grow up to be President, and you even get re-elected, that's still only eight years. What do you do with the rest of your life?" When Harry later saw the cartoon, he grabbed a pen and scrawled across the bottom, "God *only* knows!!!"

For starters, Harry and Bess became steady patrons of the Independence Public Library. Neighbors enjoying an evening walk could often see the outline of the retired couple behind their living room window, each sitting with a book under a reading lamp.

Although Harry was a voracious reader, he was the first to admit, "I'm not a writer!" So somewhat begrudgingly, he also wrote his memoirs during his retirement. One book, about his first twelve months in office, was called *Year of Decisions;* the other, *Years of Trial and Hope,* was about his remaining time in the White House. "How much is lost to us because so few Presidents have told their own stories," Harry wrote in the introduction to his memoirs.

Dearest to Harry's heart was his presidential library. The Harry S Truman Library was constructed just a few blocks from his home on a quiet, scenic, thirteen-acre town park. "All partisanship and selfishness were left behind months ago and this home city of this world famous statesman is the most logical place to establish such a national shrine as the Harry S Truman Library," wrote the *Kansas City Times.* It housed books, presidential papers, official photographs, gifts, souvenirs, political cartoons, and even a model of the Oval Office, furnished as it had been during his White House years.

When you've done the best you can, you can't do any better.

—Harry Truman

For this great student of history, Harry's library became his raison d'être. He especially enjoyed sharing lessons from American history with children visiting his library. "The old folks … they're too set in their ways and too stubborn to learn anything new," explained Harry, "but I want the children to know what we've got here in this country and how we got it, and then if they want to go ahead and change it, why, that's up to them."

> Today there are eleven presidential libraries scattered all across the nation, housing the historical papers and records of all the presidents since Herbert Hoover. For a complete listing of the libraries and their locations, visit www.archives.gov/ and click on *Presidential Libraries.*

Of course, many people said the most interesting item on display at the Truman Library was Harry himself. He was there almost every day, including Sundays, sorting through papers, poring over the daily newspapers, writing letters, reading books from his vast collection, working on his memoirs, and even answering the phone early mornings before the staff arrived. "This is the old man himself," he explained to startled callers wanting to know what hours the library was open.

Well into his eighties, Harry remained active and in good spirits. Once, when a book publisher saw him sitting in a chair in his hotel room with several new books stacked on his bedside table, he asked if the president liked to read himself to sleep at night. "No, young man," responded Harry. "I like to read myself awake."

I always remember an epitaph which is in the cemetery at Tombstone, Arizona. It says: "Here lies Jack Williams. He done his damnedest." I think that is the greatest epitaph a man can have.

—Harry Truman

Harry died at age eighty-eight, in Independence. This most humble of men chose not to lie in state in Washington, D.C., with all its pomp and circumstance but instead opted for the quiet courtyard of the Truman Library, where thousands of local citizens could file past his flag-draped coffin. "I want to be out there so I can get up and walk into my office if I want to," he had once joked.

* * *

Several years after Harry's death, his daughter, Margaret, was asked what her father's idea of heaven would be. "Oh," she said, "to have a good comfortable chair, a good reading lamp, and lots of good books around that he wanted to read." Ah yes. That would be Harry's idea of heaven.

Going the Extra Mile:
Extension Activities for Harry S Truman

I. Presidential Trivia

Okay, trivia buffs. There are lots of fun facts about the presidents and their strange pets, favorite foods, silly nicknames, unusual hobbies, and goofy personality traits. But what about their reading habits? What about books they wrote and libraries they built? Here's a little trivia focusing on the literary lives of our presidents.

Which President …

1. Received no formal education and was taught to read and write by his wife?

2. Was the fastest reader, recorded at 2,000 words per minute?

3. Created the first permanent library at the White House?

4. Had a photographic memory, remembering every single word appearing on a page of text?

5. Did not learn to read until he was nine years old but later went on to earn his law degree and doctor of philosophy (Ph.D.) in political science?

6. Was farsighted in one eye and nearsighted in the other but still managed to read without glasses?

7. Did not even mention his wife's name when he wrote his autobiography?

8. Won a Pulitzer Prize for his book titled *Profiles in Courage*?

9. Sold his collection of some 7,000 books to Congress for $23,000, the volumes later forming the basis of the Library of Congress in Washington, D.C.?

10. Was thrilled when his proof of the Pythagorean Theorem was published in a book with 369 other outstanding mathematical proofs?

11. Finished his memoirs just a few weeks before his death, never realizing that they would become a best-seller and even be considered among the greatest of military memoirs?

12. Conjures up the indelible image of a boy sitting on the dirt floor of a log cabin reading all alone by the glow of the firelight?

Answers: 1. Andrew Johnson. 2. Jimmy Carter. 3. Millard Fillmore. 4. Theodore Roosevelt. 5. Woodrow Wilson. 6. James Buchanan. 7. Martin Van Buren. 8. John F. Kennedy. 9. Thomas Jefferson. 10. James Garfield. 11. Ulysses S. Grant. 12. Abraham Lincoln.

II. Sadako and the Thousand Paper Cranes

When Harry Truman made the decision to drop an atomic bomb on Hiroshima, two-year-old Sadako Sasaki was living just one mile from Ground Zero. Initially unscathed by the bombing, she grew into a strong and athletic girl who loved to run on her school's track team. But then tragedy struck. In 1954, while training for a race, she suddenly became dizzy and collapsed to the ground. She was diagnosed with leukemia, also known as the "atom bomb disease," brought on by her exposure to the radiation from the atomic bomb some ten years earlier.

While hospitalized, Sadako's best friend told her of an old Japanese legend which said that anyone who folded a thousand origami paper cranes would be granted one wish. So began Sadako's quest to fold a thousand paper cranes, one by one, mostly out of her medicine bottle wrappers. By doing so, she not only hoped that the gods would make her well; she prayed for peace and healing to all the innocent victims of the atomic bomb.

Sadly, Sadako fell short of her goal, folding 644 paper cranes before her tragic death at the age of twelve. But happily, the story does not end there. Inspired by Sadako's strength and courage, her friends and classmates completed the remaining 356 paper cranes and buried them with her. They also published a collection of letters to raise funds to build a memorial to Sadako and all of the children who died from the atomic bomb in Hiroshima. In 1958, a statue of Sadako holding a golden crane was unveiled at Hiroshima's Peace Park. At the foot of the statue is a plaque which reads, *This is our cry. This is our prayer. Peace in the world.*

Sadako's inspiring story has become familiar to schoolchildren all over the world through Eleanor Coerr's novel, *Sadako and the Thousand Paper Cranes.* Read it. Then pay tribute to Sadako and all the children who died from the atomic bomb dropped on Hiroshima by joining your friends and classmates in folding a thousand paper cranes. (To learn how, visit www.sadako.com/howtofold.html.) When you have completed the thousand paper cranes, strung on garlands of one hundred cranes each, mail them to:

Office of the Mayor

City of Hiroshima

6-34 Kokutaiji-Machi

1 Chome Naka-ku, Hiroshima 730

Japan

In this way, your thousand paper cranes will be displayed at Hiroshima's Peace Park along with ten million other cranes offered each year before Sadako's statue.

III. Whistle Stop Campaign

President Harry Truman during a whistle stop campaign speech, 1948

Even though Harry Truman stumbled into the presidency when Franklin Delano Roosevelt suddenly died in office, he tried to "keep [his] job" during his hard-fought 1948 presidential campaign against the Republican candidate Thomas Dewey. Over the course of four months Harry traveled some 22,000 miles aboard a train, giving his trademark whistle stop campaign speeches from the rear platform. The strategy worked. Despite the fact that the national press was nearly unanimous in predicting a Dewey victory, and almost all the public opinion polls showed Dewey the frontrunner, Harry pulled off what is still widely considered to be the biggest political upset in American history.

Your assignment is to pretend you are Harry Truman, addressing an audience of local townspeople during a whistle stop in the Midwest. Your speech should be two to four minutes in length, using note cards and some sort of prop (thick-lensed glasses, a business suit with a lapel, Harry's trademark hat or cap, etc.). You can pick any topic your heart desires, although it must accurately reflect Harry's political viewpoint and include at least five relevant facts gleaned from library books or Internet research. To borrow a campaign phrase, "Give 'em hell, [kiddo]!"

References

Books and Magazines

Denotes books and magazines of special interest to middle readers.
† *Denotes sources for quotations in this chapter.*

* † Krull, Kathleen. *Lives of the Presidents: Fame, Shame (and What the Neighbors Thought)*. New York: Harcourt Brace, 1998.

† McCullough, David. *Truman*. New York, Simon & Schuster, 1992.

* † Otfinoski, Steven. *Harry S. Truman: Encyclopedia of Presidents*. New York: Childrens Press, 2005.

* Schuman, Michael A. *Harry S. Truman*. Springfield, NJ: Enslow, 1997.

* St. George, Judith. *So You Want to Be President?* New York: Philomel Books, 2000.

Additional Resources

Web Sites

Truman Presidential Museum and Library: www.trumanlibrary.org. Check out the museum's many special exhibits as well as extensive archives.

The American Presidency: http://ap.grolier.com. Find brief biographies of all the presidents from several online encyclopedias.

Presidential Inaugural Addresses: http://www.bartleby.com/124/pres53.html. Read Harry's inaugural address in its entirety as well as the inaugural addresses of all of the other presidents.

The White House: http://www.whitehouse.gov. Take a visual tour of the White House and find trivia quizzes, current events questions, and much more.

Places to Visit in Missouri

Harry S Truman Birthplace State Historic Site in Lamar. Harry's birthplace and where he lived the first year of his life.

Harry S Truman Farm House in Grandview. The home where Harry lived and worked on the farm from 1906 to 1917.

Harry S Truman National Historic Site in Independence. With the exception of their years in the White House, this is the home where Harry and Bess lived throughout their marriage.

Truman Presidential Museum and Library in Independence. See presidential papers, official photographs, gifts, souvenirs, political cartoons, and even a model of the Oval Office furnished as it had been during Truman's White House years.

Videos

Truman. PBS Home Video, 2006.

Truman. Soundworks, 2006.

Truman: A Simple Man, A Legendary President. HBO Home Video, 1995.

Illustration Credits

In the order photos appear in this chapter: 1. Wikipedia. 2. Wikipedia. 3. Wikipedia. 4. Wikipedia. 5. Wikipedia. 6. Wikipedia. 7. Wikipedia. 8. Dr. William J. Ball, Department of Political Science, The College of New Jersey.

Norman Rockwell

1894—1978

Norman Rockwell

Have you ever seen a painting by Norman Rockwell? Known as the People's Painter, *he's one of the most popular of American artists. He is also regarded as one of America's greatest storytellers. That's because Norman's paintings were really spellbinding stories, with each stroke of his paintbrush adding fresh details to the plot. You know the expression, "a picture is worth a thousand words." Well, the same might be said about Norman's illustrations. As you will see, it is astonishing just how much Norman's simple, everyday pictures could "say" without using a single word.*

Much of what Norman tried to convey was about real people doing simple, ordinary things. Through his paintings, he captured the everyday pleasures that can otherwise slip by if we don't pause for a moment and appreciate them. "The commonplaces of America are to me the richest subjects in art," Norman once said. "Boys batting flies on vacant lots; little girls playing jacks on the front steps; old men plodding home at twilight, umbrellas in hand—all of these things arouse feelings in me. Commonplaces never become tiresome. It is we who become tired when we cease to be curious and appreciative."

Norman's paintings struck an emotional chord with America. Much like the long lines that form in bookstores today, awaiting the next installment in J. K. Rowling's Harry Potter series, there was great anticipation during Norman's day for the most recent issue of the Saturday Evening Post *with his cover on it. After each new issue hit the newsstands, admiring fan mail poured into his studio.*

Norman's popularity reached its highest point during World War II. His inspiring paintings of the Four Freedoms *(based on President Franklin Roosevelt's address outlining the four basic freedoms to which all people are entitled: freedom of speech, freedom of worship, freedom from want, and freedom from fear) united the nation behind the war effort and raised a whopping $132 million in war bonds. As Norman humbly explained, "I was showing the America I knew and observed to others who might not have noticed."*

Norman later attributed much of his success to—you guessed it—books. He first got interested in illustrating at age eight, while listening to his father read aloud from novels by Charles Dickens. Years later, he loved painting at his easel while his wife, Mary, read aloud from the Harvard Classics. *Over the course of his career, he illustrated some forty books including the children's classics,* Adventures of Huckleberry Finn *and* Tom Sawyer. *He also featured books and bookworms on dozens of his covers for the* Saturday Evening Post, *some of which you will see here.*

To learn more about this major-league illustrator, read Beverly Gherman's Norman Rockwell: Storyteller with a Brush. *In addition, you may wish to read Norman's words and see many of his pictures in his aptly named autobiography,* My Adventures as an Illustrator.

Norman Perceval Rockwell was born in the art capital of the United States, New York City. Named after a wealthy English ancestor, he grew up in what he later described as a "shabby brownstone" at the corner of "a hundred an' toid" and Amsterdam. His father was the office manager of a textile firm by day and dabbled in art by night. His mother was frail and often sick, spending many of her days and nights on a couch with a cold towel on her head.

Norman did not exactly have the happiest of childhoods. He wore glasses that were big and round with black rims, prompting other kids to tease him and call him "Mooney." His skin was so pale his mother nicknamed him *Snow-in-the-Face*. But worst of all was his super-skinny, clumsy-looking body, a physique made all the worse by the fact that his older brother, Jarvis, was strong and athletic. "He always came in first," said Norman. "I always came in last, puffing and blowing."

To be more athletic like Jarvis, young Norman threw himself into a rigorous exercise regimen. He woke up early and pushed himself to the limit doing jumping jacks, deep-knee bends, push-ups, and sit-ups. And where did all that iron discipline get him? Sadly, nowhere. Months later, when he looked into his bedroom mirror, he still had the same ostrich-like neck, bony Adam's apple, "narrow shoulders, jelly arms, and thin measly-looking legs" he had always had.

Charles Dickens

Norman gave up his dreams of becoming a jock and turned instead to books. Each night before bedtime, his father gathered the family around the dining room table and read aloud a chapter from a Charles Dickens novel. Among the classics were *David Copperfield, Great Expectations,* and *Oliver Twist.* Even though his father's reading voice was "even and colorless," Norman's imagination soared. He could see some of the characters in the books so clearly in his head—characters such as Oliver Twist, Uriah Heep, Mr. Pickwick, and David Copperfield—he was soon sketching them in a pad at the kitchen table.

Norman had the most fun with the colorful characters in *David Copperfield.* "I'd draw Mr. Micawber's head, smudge it, erase it and start over, my tongue licking over my upper lip as I concentrated," he noted. "Then I'd ask my father to read the description of Mr. Micawber again." Already a perfectionist, Norman wanted to get his drawings just right. He was determined to sketch the characters from the book in a way that perfectly matched the author's detailed descriptions.

Norman later said he was "deeply impressed and moved by Dickens." The author not only fueled his imagination and inspired his very first illustrations but also changed the way the young artist looked at the world around him. "I became insatiably curious … and I began to look at things the way I imagined Dickens would have looked at them," Norman said. Many years later when Norman wrote his best-selling autobiography, *My Adventures as an Illustrator*, Charles Dickens's name appeared on the very first page—speaking volumes about the author's influence upon his life.

Once he started sketching Dickens's characters at the kitchen table, it didn't take long for Norman to realize he had talent. "Jarvis could jump over three orange crates; Jack Outwater had an uncle who had seen a pirate; George Dugan could wiggle his ears; I could draw," Norman said matter-of-factly. "[My] ability was just something I had, like a bag of lemon drops."

Norman's friends also caught wind of his artistic talent. They pleaded with him to draw with chalk on the sidewalk. "Draw a horse," some begged. "Draw a soldier, an automobile, a dog," others urged. He also built cardboard battleships for his friends' navy games, first sketching the ships on pieces of cardboard and then cutting them out and bending the edges to make them stand up sturdy and tall. Norman and his friends used the cardboard ships to reenact the recent battle of Manila Bay, won by Admiral George Dewey in the Spanish-American War.

From *Readers and Leaders* by Susan Steffensen Romaine. Westport, CT: Libraries Unlimited.
Copyright © 2007 Libraries Unlimited.

Norman's drawings did not just appear on cardboard and sidewalks. One of his teachers turned over all the chalkboards in her classroom at Christmas time so Norman could draw large, colorful murals to brighten up the room. Another insisted that Norman include drawings in his written reports. "Revolutionary soldiers and covered wagons for history; birds, lions, fish, elephants for science," Norman recalled.

While Norman shined in art, he felt bored by the rest of the school day. His boredom led to not only poor grades but also mischievous pranks on the principal. For one such prank (running the principal's long underwear up the school flagpole), Norman found himself suspended from school for several days.

By age fifteen, Norman decided to quit high school altogether and enter art school. In his own words, he already knew "that was what he wanted to do with his life." His mother was deeply disappointed by his decision, as she herself was the daughter of a struggling artist. "My mother thought I would end up dying of starvation in an attic," Norman remembered, "but it didn't work out that way."

It turns out that it was the perfect time to be studying art, during what came to be known as "the Golden Age of Illustration." Magazines and books did not yet have the technology to reproduce photographs, so they depended on artists to draw and paint scenes and portraits. The artists who made their careers as illustrators during this time included some of the best talent in America—N. C. Wyeth, Frederic Remington, Winslow Homer, and Howard Pyle, among others. To Norman, it was a noble profession because an illustrator was "a historian with a brush." He pored over their illustrated books and magazines and haunted the museums where their drawings and paintings were displayed.

At the Art Students League, Norman was nicknamed the "Deacon." He was very serious when he worked, refusing to let anything or anybody interfere with his concentration. His favorite class was (why, of course) illustrations. The instructor, Mr. Fogarty, pushed and prodded Norman to paint with his heart as well as his brush. "Painting a picture is like throwing a ball against a wall," Mr. Fogarty exclaimed. "Throw it hard, ball comes back hard. Feel a picture hard, public feels it the same way."

Crackers in Bed. Copyright © 1921
the Norman Rockwell Family Entities.

From *Readers and Leaders* by Susan Steffensen Romaine. Westport, CT: Libraries Unlimited.
Copyright © 2007 Libraries Unlimited. **113**

Norman followed Mr. Fogarty's advice when he painted *Crackers in Bed*. It shows a boy lying in bed with the mumps, too sick to watch the Fourth of July fireworks just outside his bedroom window. He seems comforted by his dog napping at the foot of his bed and a box of saltine crackers at his side.

Yet the spotlight shines on the book the boy is reading. Like so many good books, it has transported the boy faraway from his own worries and misfortunes, to a whole new world of fantasies and adventures. The ultimate escape! Notice the stack of books under the boy's lamp, filled with the next round of escapes for this bed-bound patient. *Crackers in Bed* told such a good story, it was recognized as the best painting of the year in Mr. Fogarty's class, the first of Norman's many honors to come.

Norman decided it was time to go out into the world for real illustrating jobs, not just classroom projects. He started off with small jobs, such as sketches for mail catalogs and medical textbooks. He labored over pen drawings in camping handbooks and calendars for the Boys Scouts of America. Finally, his first big breakthrough came when he was offered a job illustrating C. H. Claudy's popular children's book, *Tell Me Why*: *Stories about Mother Nature*.

Mark Twain

While Norman agreed it was "fun to do a really good book," he admitted that "only the best titles give me any satisfaction." That opportunity came knocking on his door when he was asked to illustrate two great children's classics, *Tom Sawyer* and *The Adventures of Huckleberry Finn*. "I was so excited," Norman remembered. "I was asked to illustrate the classics of Mark Twain. He's one of my very favorite authors. I felt so honored that they had come to me to illustrate his books. He's great!"

Norman plunged head-over-heels into his new project. He first reread both books, looking for the best sixteen scenes to paint—eight in each book. He also studied the illustrations of other artists commissioned for earlier editions of *Tom Sawyer* and *Huckleberry Finn*. Norman not only wanted his pictures to be entirely different from anything painted before, he wanted them to be so good they took on "the smell of the place." That meant traveling to Hannibal, Missouri, Twain's hometown, where Norman could see with his own eyes the actual settings of the stories. He was the first illustrator of these two children's classics to do so.

To feel the pulse of Hannibal, Norman walked down the same streets as Tom and Huck did. He climbed over the same fences, strolled into the same stores and houses, and explored the same secret cave. He even purchased for his models the same straw hats "worn in the sun and sweated in and sat on and rained on." Norman's sketchbook soon bulged with local color as he followed a teacher's advice to "Step over the frame and live in the picture."

From *Readers and Leaders* by Susan Steffensen Romaine. Westport, CT: Libraries Unlimited.
Copyright © 2007 Libraries Unlimited.

Through Huckleberry Finn and Tom Sawyer, Norman gained fame as a successful book illustrator. Still, only the very best artists were asked to produce the front cover of the *Saturday Evening Post.* Founded by Benjamin Franklin, the *Saturday Evening Post* was a monthly magazine read in millions of homes all across America. It included the latest fiction by nationally known writers, as well as articles about politics and daily living. "In those days the cover of the *Post* was … the greatest show window in America for an illustrator," said Norman. "If you did a cover for the *Post* you had arrived."

Norman not only arrived, he thrived. Beginning with his first cover at age twenty-two, he painted a record 332 *Saturday Evening Post* covers. It was hard work coming up with brand-new ideas for covers and then figuring out the best way to draw them. Yet of all the things Norman did over his lifetime, the *Post* covers were by far his favorite. They were "the first thing he thought about in the morning, and the last thing he thought about at night," one biographer said.

While painting *Post* covers, Norman liked to smoke his favorite briar pipe. He dressed casually in jeans or khakis, and a flannel shirt rolled up at the sleeves. For relaxation his wife, Mary, often read aloud to him as he sat at his easel, much as his father had done when he was a young boy sitting around the dining room table. Mary read many of the best-selling novels and biographies of the time as well as selections from the *Harvard Classics.* As Norman explained, "She went through the complete works of some of them, the complete Dickens, for one. I've always loved Dickens. And Henry James, Tolstoy, Dostoevsky. Jane Austen, too—that was a favorite of hers."

Norman often said that he painted more easily when a book was being read to him. But that's not the only reason he listened so attentively as Mary read aloud from great works in literature. He truly valued the whole learning process. For remember, Norman dropped out of high school at age sixteen to pursue art. That decision, although right for Norman at the time, left deep holes in his formal education. He took great pride in plugging those holes by reading as much as he possibly could—much like his self-educated hero, Abraham Lincoln. Norman later considered his lack of schooling "a badge of honor," since he would go on to accomplish so much without it.

The Law Student. Copyright © 1927 the Norman Rockwell Family Entities.

From Readers and Leaders by Susan Steffensen Romaine. Westport, CT: Libraries Unlimited.
Copyright © 2007 Libraries Unlimited.

Given his own passion for reading, it is not surprising that books and bookworms were a common theme in Norman's *Saturday Evening Post* covers. Take *The Law Student*. A grocery store clerk sits hunched over a cracker barrel, reading a law book by the light of a kerosene lamp. He has a serious, earnest look on his face. Notice the portraits of Abe Lincoln tacked to the wall—torn, bent, and yellowing with age. The whole scene looks old-fashioned, but for good reason. Norman seems to be saying that Abe's values of hard work and industry are timeless. He seems to be saying that *any* small-town boy (or girl), however humble his background or education, can achieve anything in life by being honest, working hard, and reading the great books. As Abe himself used to say, "Good boys who to their books apply, will be great men by and by."

Breaking Home Ties. Copyright © 1954 the Norman Rockwell Family Entities.

One of Norman's most popular *Saturday Evening Post* covers was called *Breaking Home Ties*. A boy sits with his father and dog, waiting for the train that will take him away to college. Dressed to a tee and sitting ramrod straight, he looks eagerly down the tracks for the train that marks the arrival of a new chapter in his life.

Check out the stack of books on top of his suitcase with the bookmarks resting neatly in between the pages. It seems the boy has already begun his course work, to hit the ground running when classes begin.

Now take a close look at the boy's father, perhaps a farmer. He sits with his son on the running board of a beat-up old truck, looking as worn out as his coveralls. The boy's father has obviously worked hard for this day and sacrificed so much of his own happiness it seems for that of his son. But now that the day has arrived, it pains the father to look in the direction of the train that's coming to take his son away. He fidgets with his hat brim; a cigarette hangs loosely from his mouth. Thoughts are hard to express; words are hard to come by. The family's collie looks just as sad, resting his head on the boy's knee and knowing instinctively that change is about to come.

Breaking Home Ties is a make-believe father and son, but it is based on Norman's misgivings about his own son growing up and leaving home. What Norman couldn't say in words to his son, he expressed in his paintings. It's a sad painting, but a hopeful one as well. The stack of books represents opportunity—for the son to have a shot at a better life than his father, to live by his wits rather than his hands.

For a much lighter *Post* cover, there is the *Bookworm*. Do you know what a bookworm is? Well, the literal meaning is a pesky little critter that eats through the bindings and pages of books. Some of the book "eaters" are really worms, while others may be lice or beetles.

Here's a fun puzzle for you. A bookworm eats from the first to last page of an encyclopedia. The encyclopedia consists of ten, one-thousand page volumes and is sitting on a bookcase in the usual order. If the bookworm eats in a straight line, how many pages does the bookworm eat? The answer is printed at the bottom of this page.

But you may be more familiar with a very different kind of bookworm—a *person* who devours page after page of books. Bookworms love books like some kids love Ben & Jerry's ice cream or Snickers candy bars. *Any* kind of book. A detective story, murder mystery, romance novel, sports thriller, biography, or fantasy. Science fiction, historical fiction, nonfiction. You name it. A bookworm loves it.

A bookworm reads practically anything, almost anywhere. In a cold attic or a steamy bath tub. In a cozy lounge chair or on a hard bleacher seat. In a noisy school bus or on a quiet airplane. Standing in a grocery store line or sitting in a dentist's waiting room. I've even seen an eleven-year-old bookworm reading while walking to and from school each day. He's what you call a *Walking Encyclopedia*!

In his painting called *Bookworm*, Norman captures a reader's addiction to books. A rather disheveled and absent-minded man (notice he is wearing two different shoes) reads with his proverbial nose in a book while standing at a used book sale. Several books are tucked under his arm and who knows how many more books are already in his wicker basket. In other words, he just can't get enough! This whole scene brings a smile to book lovers everywhere, which is why it is often displayed on bookmarks.

Bookworm. Copyright © 1926 the Norman Rockwell Family Entities.

Last but certainly not least, *The Problem We All Live With* is a great example of a painting that speaks ten thousand words. An eight-year-old, African American girl named Ruby Bridges is walking to school wearing white tennis shoes, white socks, a crisp white dress, and white ribbons in her pigtails. She appears to be a picture of innocence dressed from head to toe in white, clutching her school books, pencils, and ruler.

The Problem is that Ruby is unknowingly embroiled in a painful, behind-the-scenes national controversy. At the time of Norman's painting, the civil rights movement was gaining momentum, and communities all across the country were becoming more and more polarized. Angry mobs resisted court-ordered integration allowing African Americans to attend all-white schools. Norman's painting contrasts the ugly mood of the day (the word *nigger* and the initials *KKK* are scrawled on the wall) with the innocence of children like Ruby.

Solution to Bookworm Puzzle: The answer is 8,000. It may help to draw a picture of the ten volumes of encyclopedias. Notice that the first page of volume 1 is next to volume 2, and the last page of volume 10 is next to volume 9, so these two volumes go uneaten.

The Problem We All Live With. Copyright © 1964
the Norman Rockwell Family Entities.

Did you notice how your eyes zoom in on the books, pencils, and ruler that Ruby is clutching in her hand? Something as simple as a school book takes on a much bigger meaning in this painting. Some say prejudice is fed by ignorance. What we don't know, we fear. Likewise, the more we learn about different races, religions, and values, the more tolerant we tend to be of one another's differences. In short, the more we understand what makes people "tick," the more accepting we are of them—and vice versa. Books, then, not only open our minds. They open our hearts, too.

* * *

Norman Rockwell just went on painting and painting and painting. "I must work or I'll go back to being pigeon-toed, narrow-shouldered—a lump," he once joked. He typically painted ten to twelve hours a day, seven days a week. Even on Christmas, Norman would pause to open presents with his family, but then he'd be right back in his studio again. His son, Peter, remembered just one family vacation the whole time he was growing up, to Cape Cod. While the rest of the family looked around the island for a cottage to rent, Norman hunted for a studio where he could paint.

With such a strong work ethic, it's not surprising that Norman is now considered one of the most prolific artists of all time, producing over four thousand original works. He painted more than five hundred magazine covers, illustrated some forty books, and produced hundreds of calendars for organizations such as the Boys Scouts of America. He designed posters with patriotic themes during World War II. He even created advertisements for products such as Crest toothpaste, Orange Crush, and Jell-O. The list goes on and on.

Even into his eighties, Norman visited his studio every day, sometimes in his wheelchair. He admitted he sometimes painted from "fatigue to fatigue," but still he worked. Asked one day why artists tend to live such long lives, he explained: "Every painting is a new adventure. So, you see, they're always looking ahead to something new and exciting. The secret is not to look back." That's a good secret for all of us to remember.

Norman died quietly at his home "of being eighty-four," his wife said. On his easel in his studio was an unfinished canvas. And attached to that easel was a placard that read, "100%"—a reminder for Norman to always give his all to his paintings. For over seven decades he did exactly that.

It was once said of Norman that he "was as much at ease painting kings, statesmen, and movie stars as he was painting freckled-faced boys, pigtailed girls, kindly old folks and loveable dogs." Today his paintings at the Metropolitan Museum of Art in New York City, the Corcoran Gallery in Washington, D.C., and the Norman Rockwell Museum in Stockbridge, Massachusetts, are enjoyed by everyone under the sun. Norman would have wanted it no other way.

Going the Extra Mile:
Extension Activities for Norman Rockwell

I. A Picture Is Worth a Thousand Words

Norman Rockwell was commissioned to paint his very first *Saturday Evening Post* cover in 1916 at the age of twenty-two. Over the next five decades, he painted an astounding 332 covers for the *Post*, becoming a household name in the process. He depicted world events and people of his time including Charles Lindbergh's flight across the Atlantic Ocean, the soldiers of World War II, and children during the early days of school integration, as well as more intimate family scenes such as a Thanksgiving dinner, a visit to the doctor's office, and a car ride to the country.

You can see many of Norman's *Saturday Evening Post* covers by visiting the Norman Rockwell Museum Web site at www.nrm.org and clicking on *Exhibitions*. Select just one cover, and using your full imagination, write a narrative story from the perspective of just one character. What events lead up to the picture, and what events follow? What are the character's thoughts and feelings about the situation in which he or she has been placed? Is your character trying to convey a certain message? Put your picture to the test: see if you can write about a thousand words.

II. The Four Freedoms

In 1941, President Franklin Delano Roosevelt delivered his historic "Four Freedoms" speech outlining the reasons the free world was fighting in World War II: to protect each individual's right to freedom of speech and worship, as well as freedom from want and fear. Although the speech was widely praised, Norman thought the president used words that were too "darned high blown" for most Americans. The artist wondered if the president's words could be turned into pictures that would more clearly convey a message.

Tossing and turning in bed one night, Norman suddenly remembered how his neighbor had once stood up in the middle of a town meeting to voice his opinion. No one especially liked what he had to say, but they listened anyway. Now that was freedom of speech, Norman realized. He would paint that image as one of the freedoms, and then try to show the other three freedoms in the same down-to-earth, concrete way.

For *Freedom of Worship*, Norman painted a montage of heads and praying hands. *Freedom from Want* was depicted by a family gathered around a Thanksgiving table. To illustrate *Freedom from Fear*, he showed a father clutching a newspaper with the heading, "WOMEN AND CHILDREN SLAUGHTERED BY RAIDS" as he and his wife checked on their two sleeping children. Taken together, Norman thought the four paintings "showed average people doing average things," and that was how he could "portray the loftiest ideas."

You can see the powerful *Four Freedoms* display by visiting www.archives.gov/ exhibits/powers_of_persuasion/four_freedoms/four_freedoms.html, a National Archives Web site with poster art from World War II. After viewing Norman's artwork, your assignment is to design a poster based on a fifth freedom to which every American is entitled—such as freedom to assemble, or freedom from cruel and unusual punishment. To get some more ideas, it may help to read the U.S. Constitution's Bill of Rights. Your poster should be as Normanesque as possible, using a commonplace scene to portray a lofty ideal. And just like Norman, be sure to give it your all.

III. April Fool's Fun

After all the hard work and serious thought that went into the *Four Freedoms* illustrations, Norman decided it was time to do something a little lighter for his *Saturday Evening Post* covers. That's when he came up with the idea for his first of three April Fool's Day designs, the artist's tongue-and-check response to people who had written to him over the years pointing out mistakes with props and costumes in his covers. For the April Fool's Day illustrations, Norman intentionally painted many of his props upside down and backward and his scenery as surreal as possible. For example, a cat may have the head of a dog and the tail of a raccoon; or ivy may be growing around a hot potbellied stove.

To take a close look at *April Fool: Checkers*, visit www.nrm.org, and click on *Exhibitions*. Or you can find the painting in one of the many books about Norman Rockwell. In the topsy-turvy world depicted in *April Fool: Checkers*, a couple is playing a game of chess while geese fly through the living room, a skunk rests on the woman's lap, a deer lounges underneath the man's chair, and mushrooms grow out of the carpet. Believe it or not, there are forty-one more mistakes that Norman deliberately drew in this practical joke, of sorts. See how many you can find.

Answers to April Fool's Fun (from *Cobblestone* magazine's December 1989 issue)

Easier mistakes to find: fish on stairway, water on stairway, mailbox in house, faucet at side of fireplace, wallpaper pattern behind faucet is upside-down, woodpecker pecking woman's chair, mushrooms growing out of carpet, woman's dress with back pocket, newspaper in her back pocket, small silhouette pictures on wall hung upside-down, scissors used as candleholders, plate with bacon and egg on mantelpiece, clock on mantel has April Fool for numbers, portraits have man coming out of picture, mouse's head popping out of mantelpiece, two ducks flying across scene, crown on woman's head, skunk on woman's lap, woman holding wrench for a nutcracker in her hand, woman wearing pants under her dress, woman wearing pants under her dress, woman wearing ice skates, glass and medicine bottle floating in air, wallet attached to string which is attached to man's finger, bird in man's pocket, man wearing a dress, man wearing roller skates, man with hoe for a cane, deer under man's chair, plants growing out of the carpet, milk bottles growing out of plants, zebra looking out of picture frame, artist's signature written backward.

Harder mistakes to find: fishhook in front of fish on stairway, stairway behind fireplace (which Norman claimed was architecturally impossible), two different patterns of wallpaper, buttons on wrong side of woman's sweater, woman's wedding ring on wrong hand, wrong number of squares on checkerboard, no checkers on checkerboard, pencil behind man's ear with eraser on both ends, tire forming rim of fireplace, fork instead of spoon on top of medicine bottle, too many fingers on man's hand, buckle on man's slipper, deer with dog's paws.

From *Readers and Leaders* by Susan Steffensen Romaine. Westport, CT: Libraries Unlimited.

References

Books and Magazines

* Denotes books and magazines of special interest to middle readers.

† Denotes sources for quotations in this chapter.

* Finch, Christopher. *Norman Rockwell's 332 Magazine Covers*. New York: Abbeville Press, 1995.

* Finch, Christopher. *Norman Rockwell's America*. New York: Harry N. Abrams, 1975.

* † Gherman, Beverly. *Norman Rockwell: Storyteller with a Brush*. New York: Atheneum Books for Young Readers, 2000.

* Guptill, Arthur L. *Norman Rockwell, Illustrator*. New York: Watson-Guptill, 1971 (reprinting).

* Hennessey, Maureen Hart, and Knutson, Anne. *Norman Rockwell: Pictures for the American People*. New York: Harry N. Abrams, 1999.

* † Rockwell, Norman. *My Adventures as an Illustrator as Told to Thomas Rockwell*. Garden City, NY: Doubleday, 1960.

* † Yoder, Carolyn P. *Cobblestone's Norman Rockwell*. Peterborough, NH: Cobblestone Publishing. December 1989 issue.

Additional Resources

Web Sites

Norman Rockwell Museum: www.nrm.org. Among the highlights found here are Norman's *Saturday Evening Post* covers and the widely popular *Four Freedoms* series.

The Golden Age of Illustrations: www.artcyclopedia.com/history/golden-age.html. A survey of the leading illustrators and their works during the Golden Age.

Places to Visit

Norman Rockwell Museum in Stockbridge, Massachusetts. This museum houses the world's largest collection of original Rockwell art.

National Scouting Museum in Murray, Kentucky. Among the fifty-four Rockwell originals at this museum are many of the artist's paintings for *Boys Life* and for *Boy Scout* calendars.

National Air and Space Museum, Smithsonian Institution, in Washington, D.C. On display are some of Norman's paintings of the American space program, including Neal Armstrong taking his first step on the moon.

Mark Twain's Boyhood Home and Museum in Hannibal, Missouri. Some of Norman's paintings used to illustrate *Tom Sawyer* and *The Adventures of Huckleberry Finn* are displayed here.

Videos

Biography—Norman Rockwell. A&E Home Video, 2006.

Norman Rockwell—Painting America. An American Masters production by Winstar, 1999.

American Masters—The Artists, Winstar, 2004.

Illustration Credits

In the order photos appear in this chapter: 1. Wikipedia. 2. Perry-Castaneda Library. 3. Walnet Institute and Norman Rockwell Family Agency. 4. Wikimedia Commons. 5. PK Imaging and Norman Rockwell Family Agency. 6. Curtis Publishing and Norman Rockwell Family Agency. 7. Curtis Publishing and Norman Rockwell Family Agency. 8. Norman Rockwell Museum and Norman Rockwell Family Agency.

Anne Frank

1929–1945

Anne Frank

Do you keep a diary? Lots of kids do. The most famous one ever written is The Diary of a Young Girl *by Anne Frank. Anne wrote it as a teenager, while hiding from the Nazis in a secret apartment during World War II. What makes the diary so special is the way Anne talked about her extraordinary life—blending details of her time in hiding (bland food, shabby clothing, cramped rooms, fussy roommates, and endless boredom) with all the swings of emotion of a typical teenaged girl. Her diary, named Kitty, was Anne's best friend, and writing was her greatest source of comfort. "When I write I can shake off all my fears," she wrote.*

Besides writing in her diary, Anne relaxed by reading books. For two years she was not allowed to step foot outside her secret hiding place—not even once—for fear that she would be discovered and sent to a Nazi concentration camp. In short, she lived much like a prisoner confined to a cell, where books and magazines were her only means of escape. Thanks to workers in a warehouse below her hiding place, a steady stream of reading materials was smuggled to Anne. Whether they were fluffy romance novels and fashion magazines or thick histories and biographies, they all helped to push Anne's worries aside and free her mind to travel to worlds miles and miles beyond the walls of her hiding place. "Ordinary people simply don't know what books mean to us, shut up here," she wrote.

Throughout it all, Anne craved simple pleasures that most every teenager takes for granted. "Cycling, dancing, whistling, looking out into the world, feeling young, to know that I'm free—that's what I long for." Despite her trials and tribulations, Anne kept her chin up and tried to make the best out of the very worst of circumstances. In perhaps the most frequently quoted line from her diary, she wrote: "In spite of everything, I still believe that people are really good at heart." Her spirit of eternal optimism continues to inspire those who read her diary and learn her life story. So, let us begin …

From *Readers and Leaders* by Susan Steffensen Romaine. Westport, CT: Libraries Unlimited.
Copyright © 2007 Libraries Unlimited.

Wednesday, 12 June 1929

Annelies Marie Frank was born into a Jewish family in Frankfurt, Germany. Her parents were Otto and Edith, and her older sister was Margot. When Otto registered the birth of his daughter and stated her full name, the clerks at the hospital were befuddled. Annelies Marie? They had recorded *infant Frank* as a boy. The baby's ears stuck out almost comically, and she had a mane of silky black hair. But her most notable feature was her strong will. "Has been screaming all night for the past six weeks," Edith wrote in her baby book. Thankfully, the crying stopped, and Anne spent her afternoons playing happily in a sandbox with children from the neighborhood.

Friday, 30 June 1933

Outside the playful world of Anne's sandbox, bad things were happening in Germany. Many Germans had lost their jobs and had no money for essential food and clothing. Scared and angry, they were looking for a leader who promised a swift end to their problems. Adolf Hitler gained in popularity by telling the German people that they were the strongest and fittest people on earth and by blaming all their troubles on the Jews. "The Jews are our scourge," Hitler said.

Adolf Hitler

Sadly, many Germans bought into Hitler's message, and on the day of this journal entry, he was elected their chancellor. The result was predictable. Jews were isolated, meaning that non-Jews stopped visiting Jews in their homes and started sitting apart from them in classrooms and public spaces. Nazis hung signs in front of Jewish shops that read *Don't Buy from Jews*. Worse still, the Nazis burned thousands and thousands of books by famous Jewish authors. "When the Jews write in German, they lie," the Nazis gave as their reason for the book burnings.

While books burned, writers disappeared. Take the popular Jewish poet Heinrich Heine. Almost all German schoolchildren knew his poem *Lorelei* by heart, but almost overnight this household name ceased to exist. Poof—just like that. Simply because he was Jewish. *Poet Unknown* replaced *Heinrich Heine* in new editions of textbooks citing his works.

Autumn 1933

The Franks' apartment in Amsterdam, Netherlands

Anne's parents felt unsafe in Nazi Germany and moved the family to nearby Amsterdam, Netherlands. It was the beginning of several carefree years. Anne had many neighborhood friends, and together they played ping-pong, hopscotch, and Monopoly. Still headstrong, Anne often insisted on having her way with friends. "God knows everything, but Anne knows everything better," one friend's mother joked.

Friday, 10 May 1940

Hitler and his German army were on the march, spreading war across Europe. It was on this day that Hitler's armies invaded the Netherlands. Anne wrote that the good times were now "few and far between." She still pursued her many interests including history, Greek mythology, writing, cats, dogs, and … oh yes, movie stars. But the dark and menacing Nazi cloud now hung over her head, as she described here:

> *There have been all sorts of Jewish laws. Jews must wear a yellow star; Jews must hand in their bicycles. Jews are banned from trams and are forbidden to use any car, even a private one; Jews are only allowed to do their shopping between three and five o'clock; and then only in shops which bear the placard Jewish Shop. Jews may only use Jewish barbers; Jews must be indoors from eight o'clock in the evening until six o'clock in the morning.*

From *Readers and Leaders* by Susan Steffensen Romaine. Westport, CT: Libraries Unlimited.

Friday, 12 June 1942

A sliver of sunlight peaked through the dark clouds on this day, Anne's thirteenth birthday. She received "masses of things" as gifts:

> *… Camera Obscura, a party game, lots of sweets, chocolates, a puzzle, a brooch,* Tales and Legends of the Netherlands *by Joseph Cohen,* Daisy's Mountain Holiday *(a terrific book), and some money. Now I can buy* The Myths of Greece and Rome—*grand!*

But the best birthday gift of all was a book, a squarish diary bound in red and light-green checkered cloth. On its back cover was a strap with a narrow metal tongue that easily snapped into a small lock on the front of the book. It was the same diary she had pointed out to her father a few days earlier in the window of a bookshop. Oh, how she had yearned for that diary the first time she laid eyes on it!

In school, Anne had many friends, yet she had always wanted "one true friend." Her diary would become her closest friend. She immediately scribbled, "I hope I shall be able to confide in you completely, as I have never been able to do in anyone before, and I hope that you will be a great support and comfort to me." Little did Anne know when she inscribed those words, just how intimate she would become with her diary through the many ups and downs, and twists and turns that life had in store for her.

After much thought, Anne finally settled on a name for her best friend: *Kitty*. From this point onward, all of Anne's diary entries began, *Dear Kitty*. Why Kitty? Because one of Anne's favorite books was *Joop ter Heul,* about a plucky and adventurous girl named Joop. Like Anne, Joop had lots of girlfriends, but her best friend was named *Kitty*.

Sunday, 5 July 1942

It was a swelteringly hot summer afternoon. Anne was, in her own words, "lying lazily reading a book on the veranda in the sunshine" when the doorbell rang. Her worst nightmare had come true. The Nazis were delivering a call-up notice for Anne's sister, Margot—that is, a notice that she should report to a labor camp where she would work long and hard hours in a factory. "Everyone knows what that means," Anne wrote. "I picture concentration camps and lonely cells … Margot is 16, would they really take girls of that age away alone?"

The Nazis would—and did. Thousands of Jewish boys and girls, and men and women, were sent to labor camps where many were abused, tortured, and even killed. This period would eventually become known as the Holocaust. It was so difficult to comprehend that many Germans believed that it could not be happening. But Otto and Edith Frank feared the worst. If Margot obeyed the Nazi order, they may never see her again. Quickly and quietly, the family planned to go into hiding in a secret apartment in Amsterdam. Anne wrote:

> *Margot and I began to pack some of our most vital belongings into a school satchel. The first thing I put in was this diary, then hair curlers, handkerchiefs, schoolbooks, a comb, old letters; I put in the craziest things with the idea that we were going into hiding. But I'm not sorry; memories mean more to me than dresses.*

What did not fit into their satchel, Anne and Margot simply wore. For no Jew would dream of walking the streets with a suitcase full of clothing, a sure sign of escape. Anne dressed as if she were "going to the North Pole," layering two vests, three pairs of pants, a dress, a skirt, a jacket, summer shorts, two pairs of stockings, lace-up shoes, a wooly cap, and a scarf.

Monday, 6 July 1942

They made it! Anne and her family moved into a secret upstairs apartment in the same building where Otto worked. There were four bedrooms, a bathroom, and an attic in the secret apartment all crowded with furniture and boxes filled with linens, clothing, bedding, and kitchen utensils.

The Franks shared the apartment with three friends who were also hiding from the Nazis—Mr. and Mrs. Van Pels and their teenaged son Peter—and later a dentist, Dr. Albert Dussel. There were eight residents in all. Little did Anne know when she first stepped into her hiding place that it would be fifteen months before she stepped outside again. Fifteen months before she breathed fresh air and felt the warmth of the sun on her skin again. Sadly, Anne and her compatriots were essentially prisoners sharing a cell, which they could not leave until either Hitler was defeated and they were liberated, or they were discovered by the Nazis—whichever came first.

Four workers in the warehouse below knew Anne and her family were hiding upstairs. They became known as *helpers,* serving as the Franks' lifeline to the outside world. Along with comforting words and news of the war, the helpers sneaked books, magazines, a radio, food, blankets, paper, and medicines into the Franks' hiding place. In fact, the helpers were the unsung heroes of this whole tragedy. Each secret delivery to Anne's apartment was an act of courage, for if the helpers were caught by the Nazis, they, too, would most likely be put to death. Anne wrote:

> *It is amazing how much noble and unselfish work these people are doing, risking their own lives to help and save others. ... Never have we heard one word of the burden which we must certainly be to them, never has one of them complained about all the trouble we cause.*

Friday, 21 August 1942

Dear Kitty,

The entrance to our hiding place has now been properly concealed. Mr. Kraler [a helper] thought it would be better to put a cupboard in front of our door (because a lot of houses are being searched for hidden bicycles), but of course it had to be a movable cupboard that can open like a door.

The bookcase covering the entrance to the Secret Annex

From *Readers and Leaders* by Susan Steffensen Romaine. Westport, CT: Libraries Unlimited.
Copyright © 2007 Libraries Unlimited.

As the Nazis stepped up their manhunt for Jews, the Franks were careful not to leave behind even a shred of evidence as to their hiding place. A movable bookcase that could swing out on its hinges and open like a door was built to hide the stairs leading up to the secret apartment. Now called the Secret Annex, the hiding place had "truly become secret" to all but the helpers who could come and go as they pleased.

How fitting it was that a bookcase lined with books protected Anne and her family from their would-be captors. Along with creating this physical barrier from the Nazis, books offered the Frank family a mental escape from the many long and boring days, and dark and frightening nights, ahead.

Sunday, 27 September 1942

Dear Kitty,

Just had a big bust-up with Mummy for the umpteenth time; we simply don't get on together these days and Margot and I don't hit it off any too well either.

The novelty of living in the Secret Annex was wearing off. Anne felt cooped up ("I can't tell you how oppressive it is never to be able to go outdoors"). She complained about wearing the same old clothes ("… I have only one long-sleeved dress and three cardigans for the winter") and eating the same bland food ("We have eaten so many kidney beans and haricot beans that I can't bear the sight of them anymore"). She missed her bedroom in her old house and the black bicycle she used to ride to school. She longed for her friends. And she was frightened by the sounds of large rats running about the attic, burglars rummaging through the warehouse, and air raid sirens and gunfire echoing outside her window. "I creep into Daddy's bed nearly every night for comfort," she wrote.

Thursday, 1 October 1942

Dear Kitty,

We are as quiet as mice. Who, three months ago, would ever have guessed that quicksilver Anne would have to sit still for hours—and, what's more, could?

So as not to tip off the Nazis as to their hiding place, the Frank family remained so quiet during daytime hours that not even the sound of the proverbial pin dropping could be heard below. One way Anne passed the time was doing her schoolwork, using the textbooks she had tossed into her satchel during the escape. She enjoyed all of her subjects except algebra and geometry. Of her math book she wrote: "I've never loathed any other book so much as that one. … If I'm ever in a very wicked mood I'll tear the blasted thing to pieces." So it was that Anne's math homework always took a little extra prodding by her father. "Daddy is grumbling again, and threatens to take my diary away, oh insuperable horror," Anne wrote. "I'm going to have to hide it in future."

From *Readers and Leaders* by Susan Steffensen Romaine. Westport, CT: Libraries Unlimited.

Sunday, 11 July 1943

Dear Kitty,

We always long for Saturdays when our books come. Just like children receiving a present. Ordinary people simply don't know what books mean to us, shut up here. Reading, learning, and the radio are our amusements.

After a full year in hiding, books were now Anne's best escape from the boredom and isolation of her surroundings. Just "mad on books and reading," she explained. She began with the boxes of books that her father had brought along, but that wasn't nearly enough. Hundreds more were smuggled into the annex by the *helpers* who bought their books from *Como's,* a nearby bookstore and lending library.

Like everything else in the Secret Annex, the smuggled books were shared. As soon as one person finished a book, it was passed along to another. That way, everyone always had something to read. Even better, the eight residents formed a book club of sorts, discussing what they had read until late at night, in the darkness, when there was nothing else to do but wait.

Anne had a fondness for fiction, which allowed her to travel to safer, friendlier, make-believe worlds. She liked romantic, sentimental stories such as *Eva's Youth, The Assault,* and *Gone with the Wind.* Another favorite was *Het Boek vor de Jeugd,* a collection of fairy tales, short stories, and poems by authors such as Hans Christian Andersen, Jack London, and Jules Verne.

She also devoured movie magazines. "I am awfully pleased whenever Mr. Kugler [one of the helpers] brings the *Cinema and Theater* with him on Mondays," wrote Anne, "although this little gift is often called a waste of money by the less worldly members of the household."

Thursday, 27 April 1944

Dear Kitty,

At the moment I'm reading The Emperor Charles V. *…. I read fifty pages in five days; it's impossible to do more. The book has 598 pages, so now you can work out how long it will take me—and there is a second volume to follow. But very interesting!"*

The more Anne read, the more interested she became in nonfiction. Sometimes the reading was difficult to understand, but she plodded along anyway. She was especially keen on the biographies of important historical figures, such as Holy Roman Emperor Charles V and Queen Marie Antoinette of France. Through these biographies, she delved into the family trees of European kings and queens. "I have made great progress with a lot of them, as, for a long time already, I've been taking down notes from all the biographies and history books that I read; I even copy out many passages of history."

Then there were the German classics, which her father insisted she read. They were, after all, an important part of the family's heritage, and Otto was determined not to let the Nazis deprive her of that rightful education. Anne listened as her father read aloud plays by Goethe and Schiller, as well as books by Hebbel and other German writers. For a deeper faith, Edith urged Anne to read a book filled with German prayers. "They are certainly beautiful, but they don't convey much to me," Anne admitted.

Anne wrote down on index cards all the books she read in hiding. "I'm mad on Mythology and especially the Gods of Greece and Rome," Anne exclaimed. She also mentioned reading *Galileo Galilei, Palestine at the Crossroads,* passages from the Bible, books about painters such as Rubens and Rembrandt, and a biography of composer and pianist Franz Liszt called *Hungarian Rhapsody.* She mentioned twenty-six books in all, but she actually read many more. "I can hardly wait for the day that I shall be able to comb through the books in a public library," she mused.

From *Readers and Leaders* by Susan Steffensen Romaine. Westport, CT: Libraries Unlimited.
Copyright © 2007 Libraries Unlimited.

Thursday, 11 May 1944

Dear Kitty,

You've known for a long time that my greatest wish is to become a journalist someday and later on a famous writer. Whether these leanings towards greatness (or insanity?) will ever materialize remains to be seen. … I want to publish a book entitled Het Achterbuis [The Secret Annex] *after the war. Whether I shall succeed or not, I cannot say, but my diary will be a great help.*

Anne heard a radio broadcast where a government official urged Germans to keep a record of the war. He claimed that a collection of diaries and letters written during wartime would be published soon after the war ended. By now, Anne had been writing in her diary for almost two years. Surely the war would end soon, so she decided to get her diary ready for publication. She neatly recopied and edited it, cutting a few sentences here (especially some of the harsher comments about her mother) and adding a few sentences there (mostly about her crush on her roommate, Peter Van Pels). As for the name of her diary, she settled on *Het Achterbuis (The Secret Annex)*, so that it would appeal to prospective readers who might mistake it for a detective story.

Friday, 4 August 1944

On this most tragic of days, the Secret Annex was raided by the Nazis. While Anne and her compatriots nervously held their hands high, the Nazis grabbed the briefcase where Anne had stored her diary, notebooks, and loose papers; turned it upside down; and allowed its contents to spill over the floor. There, Anne's diary would remain, scattered among the possessions left behind in the ransacked rooms.

Auschwitz concentration camp

Anne and the other seven residents of the Secret Annex were sent off as prisoners to work in Nazi concentration camps such as Auschwitz. The conditions they encountered were horrific. With little clothing, food, or water, many of the prisoners around them died from frostbite, starvation, and disease. Others were tortured and killed. Finally, it was their turn. Mr. Van Pels died first, then Albert Dussell, Edith, Mrs. Van Pels, Margot, Anne, and Peter. Anne's father, Otto, was the lone survivor.

July 1945

Following the defeat of the Nazis and the end of World War II, Otto returned to Amsterdam where he lived with two of his helpers, Miep and Jan Gies. He was devastated by his loss, but determined to make the best of his life. "There is no point in wasting away in mourning, no point in brooding," he wrote in a letter to a friend. "We have to go on living, go on building. We don't want to forget, but we mustn't let our memories lead us to negativism."

On the very same day that Otto officially learned of the deaths of Anne and Margot, Miep opened her bottom desk drawer. She pulled out Anne's red and light-green checkered diary, her two notebooks, and 327 loose sheets of onionskin paper. That is, all of Anne's writings during her two years in hiding—writings that Miep had carefully scooped up from the floor of the Secret Annex, locked in her desk drawer, and kept safely, unread, for almost a year. It was now time to place the papers into their rightful hands. "Here is your daughter Anne's legacy to you," Miep tearfully said to Otto.

Otto was overwhelmed by the width and breadth of Anne's writings. He had no idea she had written so much about their life in hiding, nor was he aware that she could write so eloquently. It was all so good, should he try to have it published? Otto struggled with the decision. On the one hand, some of Anne's passages were perhaps too personal to share with the world, especially those about her mother and Peter. On the other hand, Anne's diary was undoubtedly an important historical document, and its publication would fulfill Anne's long-time dream of becoming a published writer.

Wednesday, 25 June 1947

Anne's diary, titled *Het Achterhuis,* first appeared in print in the Netherlands. The American version soon followed, renamed *The Diary of a Young Girl.* Readers everywhere found Anne's life in hiding so gripping and her writing so moving that her diary soon became an international best-seller.

* * *

Never in Anne's wildest dreams would she have guessed how many people would go on to read her words. Her diary has now been translated into more than sixty languages, and more than 25 million copies have been sold worldwide. That makes it second only to the Bible on the list of best-selling books of all time. How prophetic Anne was when she wrote these words: "I want to be useful or give pleasure to people around me who yet don't really know me. I want to go on living even after my death!"

From *Readers and Leaders* by Susan Steffensen Romaine. Westport, CT: Libraries Unlimited.
Copyright © 2007 Libraries Unlimited.

Burial site of Anne and Margot Frank

Keep Anne's spirit alive. *The Diary of a Young Girl* can be found in many middle and high school libraries, most local public libraries, and just about every bookstore. Check it out. You can also visit the U.S. Holocaust Memorial Museum in Washington, D.C., or the Anne Frank Center in New York City to learn more about Anne, her diary, and the Holocaust.

Going the Extra Mile: Extension Activities for Anne Frank

I. The Star of David

The Star of David (*Magen David* in Hebrew) was originally created as a symbol of God. In the Bible, the military hero King David did not win by his own might but with the support of the Almighty. Hence, the six points of the Star of David represented God's rule over the universe in all six directions: north, south, east, west, up, and down.

Star of David, sometimes called *Judenstern*

During the Holocaust, the Star of David took on a whole new meaning. Sadly, the Nazis forced the Jews to wear a Star of David, often yellow and inscribed with the word *Jude,* on their clothing as a way of identifying them. In this way, some 6 million Jews throughout Europe were isolated, stigmatized, concentrated in camps, deprived, starved, and ultimately murdered by the Nazis.

Today the Star of David has become the universal emblem of Judaism. The six-pointed star made from two interlocking equilateral triangles (thought to bring good luck) can be found on synagogues, menorahs, tallis bags, and tombstones. Ambulances in Israel bear the sign of the Red Star of David and the flag of Israel has a Blue Star of David planted squarely in its center. Go to www.flags.net and check it out for yourself.

There are all kinds of interesting ways to make the Star of David. Visit the Kid's Corner at http://www.caron-net.com/dec98files/dec98kid.html to get some ideas for designing a star using canvas, graph paper, cross-stitch, or a special yarn called Rachel. You can construct a window ornament in the shape of the Star of David by visiting www.billybear4kids.com/holidays/hanukkah/craft/star.htm. Or try making a Hanukkah card using tips found at www.enchantedlearning.com/crafts/hanukkah/star.

II. Anne Frank, the Writer

. . . I finally realized that I must do my schoolwork to keep from being ignorant, to get on in life, to become a journalist, because that's what I want! I know I can write . . . it remains to be seen whether I really have talent. . . . I need to have something besides a husband and children to devote myself to! . . . I want to be useful or bring enjoyment to all people, even those I've never met. I want to go on living even after my death! And that's why I'm so grateful to God for having given me this gift, which I can use to develop myself and to express all that's inside me!

When I write I can shake off all my cares. My sorrow disappears, my spirits are revived! But, and that's a big question, will I ever be able to write something great, will I ever become a journalist or a writer?

—Anne Frank, Wednesday, 5 April, 1944

Over the course of her two years in hiding, Anne regarded her diary as not merely a way to keep up her spirits during trying times but also as practice for her future career in journalism. As part of that practice, she often challenged herself to compose something beyond conventional diary entries by creating new rules for expression. Below are some references to some particularly creative entries in Anne's diary. After you read them, try to emulate her style with some writing samples of your own.

Wednesday, 4 August 1943 (*A Description of an Ordinary Day*): Here, Anne writes a detailed description of an ordinary day in hiding, including specific times when events occur. Her aim is to give the reader a behind-the-scenes look at what is happening in the world around her, namely, in her Secret Annex. Try a similar exercise by first choosing a location and then describing what is happening around you at specific intervals of time (say, for example, writing about your observations in the school cafeteria during five-minute intervals).

Monday, 9 August 1943 (*The Secret Annex Daily Timetable Continued*): Note the humorous way Anne describes the cast of characters with whom she eats dinner, and then try doing the same based on one of your family meals.

Wednesday, 18 August 1943 (*The Communal Task of the Day: Potato Peeling*): Just as Anne has done in this entry, pick one mundane activity and describe it in excruciatingly funny detail.

Thursday, 11 November 1943 (*Ode to My Fountain Pen: In Memoriam*): Anne cleverly describes the history and almost humanlike qualities of something as simple as a fountain pen. Your assignment is to do the same: write an ode to an inanimate object of your choice. To get some ideas, read some of the poet Pablo Neruda's odes to commonplace objects such as "Ode to Tomatoes" and "Ode to Salt" found at http://sunsite.dcc.uchile.cl/chile/misc/odas.html.

Tuesday, 16 May 1944 (*A Little Discussion*): To add variety to her diary, Anne transcribes what begins as a friendly conversation between Mr. and Mrs. Van pels but then unravels into an ugly discussion about the war, revealing pent-up frustrations and worries. Create your own dialogue about any topic of interest, even including stage directions if you so desire.

Tuesday, 1 August 1944 (*Little Bundle of Contradictions*): Just as Anne has done, compose a warts-and-all self-portrait that takes an honest and hard look at your vulnerable spots as well as your redeeming qualities.

From *Readers and Leaders* by Susan Steffensen Romaine. Westport, CT: Libraries Unlimited.

III. Book Burnings

Where books are burned, human beings are destined to be burned, too.

Hitler and the book burnings

Over a century after Heinrich Heine spoke these prophetic words, university students gathered in Berlin and other German cities to burn some 20,000 books either penned by Jewish writers or allegedly spreading "un-German ideas." This marked the beginning of Adolf Hitler's cleansing process, which sought to control the hearts and minds of the German people by censoring their reading materials. "The future German man will not just be a man of books, but a man of character," the Nazis proclaimed at the festive book burnings.

Among the books the Nazis threw into the roaring bonfires were those authored by Sigmund Freud, Ernest Hemingway, Albert Einstein, Upton Sinclair, Thomas Mann, Jack London, and H. G. Wells. Ironically, even some of Helen Keller's books (of which part of the royalties were donated to a fund for Germans blinded in World War I) were burned for espousing socialism.

Outraged by the book burnings, Helen wrote an open letter of protest published in the *New York Times* warning the German people that burning books would by no means eradicate ideas. Her letter read:

To the Student Body of Germany, May 9, 1933:

History has taught you nothing if you think you can kill ideas. Tyrants have tried to do that often before, and the ideas have risen up in their might and destroyed them.

You can burn my books and the books of the best minds in Europe, but the ideas in them have seeped through a million channels, and will continue to quicken other minds. I gave all the royalties of my books to the soldiers blinded in the World War with no thought in my heart but love and compassion for the German people.

Do not imagine your barbarities to the Jews are unknown here. God sleepeth not, and He will visit his Judgment upon you. Better were it for you to have a mill-stone hung round your neck and sink into the sea than to be hated and despised of all men.

From *Readers and Leaders* by Susan Steffensen Romaine.Westport, CT: Libraries Unlimited.
Copyright © 2007 Libraries Unlimited.

What does Helen mean when she writes in her very first sentence, "History has taught you nothing if you think you can kill ideas?" Through an Internet search, find some other examples of book burnings in history and explain how ideas have "risen up in their might" and triumphed over censorship.

Of course, even today school districts all across America struggle with the issue of censorship. In Gwinnett County, Georgia, for example, there is an effort to pull the world's most popular wizard, Harry Potter, from the shelves of school libraries. Why? Some parents argue that school-age children cannot tell fantasy from reality and will experiment with casting spells on classmates. They also contend that Harry contributes to violence and indoctrinates kids in the Wicca religion. Do you agree or disagree with those parents? Write a one-page persuasive essay on whether the Harry Potter books should be pulled from your school library.

From *Readers and Leaders* by Susan Steffensen Romaine. Westport, CT: Libraries Unlimited.

References

Books and Magazines

*Denotes books and magazines of special interest to middle readers.

†Denotes sources for quotations in this chapter.

* † Frank, Anne. *The Diary of a Young Girl* (translated from the Dutch by B.M. Mooyaart-Doubleday). New York: Bantam Books, 1967.

* Lee, Carol Ann. *Anne Frank's Story: Her Life Retold for Children*. Mahwah, NJ: Troll, 2002.

* † Sawyer, Kem Knapp. *Anne Frank*. New York: DK Publishing, 2004.

Additional Resources

Books

Lowry, Lois. *Number the Stars*. New York: Bantam Doubleday Dell Books for Young Readers, 1989. In this Newberry Award–winning novel, the friendship between two girls and the bravery of their families save the lives of a Danish Jewish family.

Schroeder, Peter W., and Schroeder-Hildebrand, Dagmar. *Six Million Paper Clips: The Making of a Children's Holocaust Memorial*. To put the Holocaust in perspective, a middle school in Tennessee collects six million paper clips (inspired by the Norwegians who wore paper clips on their lapels to protest the Nazis). The paper clips are stored in an authentic German railcar outside the school, which today serves as a Children's Holocaust Memorial.

Wiesel, Elie. *Night*. New York: Bantam Books, 1982. This is a first-person account of a teenaged boy's incarceration in the Auschwitz and Buchenwald death camps and his struggle to find meaning in the horror.

Web Sites

Anne Frank the Writer: An Unfinished Story: www.ushmm.org/museum/exhibit/online/af/htmlsite/. See more of Anne's original writings—including short stories, fairy tales, and essays, through both sounds and images.

Galleries of Holocaust Images: http://fcit.usf.edu/holocaust/resource/gallery/gallery.htm. The pictures say a thousand words.

Places to Visit

Anne Frank House in Amsterdam, Netherlands. The house where Anne Frank hid for over two years opened as a museum in 1960 and displays many important family artifacts, including Anne's original diary.

Anne Frank Center, USA, in New York City. The center introduces visitors to the history of the Holocaust while helping young people challenge prejudice and intolerance through educational programs.

Holocaust Memorial in Washington, D.C. This museum serves as the nation's memorial to all the Jews murdered during the Holocaust, receiving almost 2 million visitors a year.

New England Holocaust Memorial in Boston. Initiated by survivors of the Holocaust, this memorial features six tall, glass towers set on a black granite path. Under the towers are dark chambers representing the six death camps.

Videos

Anne Frank Remembered. Sony Pictures, 1995.

Biography—Anne Frank: The Life of a Young Girl. A&E Home Video, 2004.

Anne Frank—The Whole Story. Walt Disney Video, 2001.

Illustration Credits

In the order photos appear in this chapter: 1. Wikipedia. 2. Wikipedia. 3. Wikipedia. 4. Wikipedia. 5. Wikipedia. 6. Wikipedia. 7. Wikipedia. 8. United States Holocaust Memorial Museum.

Afterword

While writing this book in the spring of 2005, I was asked by the assistant principal of our daughter Catherine's elementary school to read books and short stories to a handful of third graders getting ready to make the big leap to fourth grade. It was an offer I could not refuse.

One morning, as we gathered around a table in the school library, I opened a book I had brought from home—a book that had been sitting on my son's bookcase for many years. It was called *Hey! Listen to This: Stories to Read Aloud,* a wonderful collection of folk and fairy tales, biographies, children's classics, animal stories, and adventures. As I flipped through the pages, I suddenly came upon my dad's handwriting. This is what he had penned on the very first page of *Stories to Read Aloud* upon our son's graduation from his first year of preschool:

> *Andrew—*
> *Congratulations on your first graduation*
> *May you have many, many more equally pleasant.*
> *Grandpa/Grandma*
> *May 30, 1995*

I paused after reading the date. My dad had autographed the book *exactly* one decade earlier—one decade to the very day—earlier. An image of his face, with his glasses still resting crooked on his nose, suddenly flashed before me. "Pull up a chair," I wanted to say, "and join our little reading group."

Index

About the Author

SUSAN STEFFENSEN ROMAINE has worked in the fields of public policy and education. She lives in Chapel Hill, North Carolina, with her husband, Craig, and their three children, Andrew, Catherine, and Natnael.

The author's royalties from the sale of *Readers and Leaders* will go to Ethiopia Reads, a not-for-profit organization developing readers and leaders by building as many as 100 free public libraries in Addis Ababa and accross the country.